EnviroThink™

to protect the environment

The Exemplary Worker Book Series

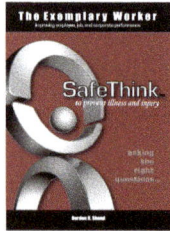

SafeThink™ ...to prevent illness and injury

SafeThink is a structured critical thinking strategy you can use to identify, predict, and control hazardous situations before, during, and after completing work. This cognitive-based safety strategy can be used on the fly, at work, at home, at play, and while driving. *SafeThink* also provides strategies for you to remain focused on your tasks.

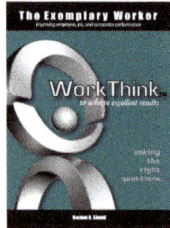

WorkThink™ ...to achieve excellent results

WorkThink is a thinking strategy you can use to achieve quality results with the least amount of effort. It usually takes little extra effort to do quality work instead of inferior work. *WorkThink* also emphasizes understanding the expectations of your supervisor, team leader, and customers so that you can achieve the excellent results they expect.

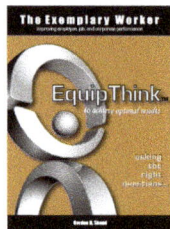

EquipThink™ ...to achieve optimal results

EquipThink is a thinking strategy for you to use tools, mobile equipment, and stationary equipment effectively and efficiently. The goals are for you to achieve the desired results with minimal stress on equipment, to conserve energy, and to extend equipment life. The input–process–output thinking strategy, in conjunction with identifying critical variables, is used to achieve optimal results.

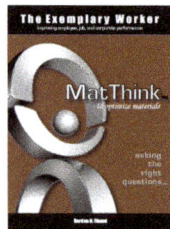

MatThink™ ...to optimize materials

MatThink is a thinking strategy you can use to make the most effective use of materials. The thinking strategy applies to recovering, processing, modifying, applying, transporting, and storing materials. Because equipment and materials are usually closely related, the input–process–output thinking strategy, in conjunction with identifying critical variables, is used to optimize material recovery and use.

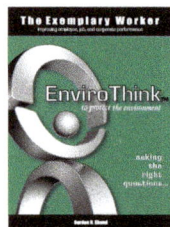

EnviroThink™ ...to protect the environment

Both industry and individuals have a responsibility to protect the environment. *EnviroThink* is a critical thinking strategy you can use to identify and respond to environmental issues for any job position that you might hold. *EnviroThink* helps you think through your work by asking yourself specific questions relating to environmental issues important to organizations.

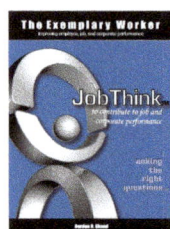

JobThink™ ...to contribute to job and corporate performance

Exemplary workers understand what is important to their organizations. They know the issues critical to business success and where to focus their efforts. *JobThink* addresses the critical thinking strategies you can use to identify what is important for job and corporate performance.

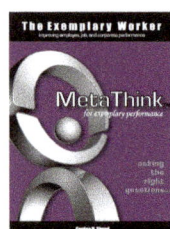

MetaThink™ ...for exemplary performance

MetaThink applies some of the thinking strategies addressed in previous books in different ways and also addresses new thinking strategies useful for the workplace. You can use these thinking strategies, along with the detailed thinking strategies addressed in other books of this series, to achieve exemplary performance.

The Exemplary Worker Book Series

Rarely can workers from any sector access self-paced instructional materials that are easy-to-use, step-by-step guides to workplace learning. *The Exemplary Worker* book set is an exception. These books offer a good breadth of learning for workers in contexts ranging from: exemplary performance; job and corporate performance; results optimization; and work excellence. With meticulous organization, these essential training references are helpful guides for workers seeking to improve their performance. With prefaces designed to help trainers/instructors assist workplace learners, these books use critical thinking strategies that identify what matters to workers and supervisors considering people, equipment, materials, environments, and organization in concert."

—**Eugene G. Kowch, Ph.D.**, Leading Complex and Adaptive Learning Systems/Organizations, University of Calgary, Canada

The power of thinking in determining our safety, health, and welfare is obvious, but how to manage such cognition or self-talk for injury prevention, self-motivation, and self-improvement is not so obvious. Answers are provided in this action-focused series of self-help books on *The Exemplary Worker* by Gordon D. Shand. He offers much practical information for leadership, safety, and well-being. Each of these books provides critical and structured thinking strategies for optimizing performance on several fronts, from improving safety and productivity in the workplace to actively caring as a teacher, parent, or friend."

—**E. Scott Geller, Ph.D.**, author of The Psychology of Safety Handbook; Alumni Distinguished Professor, Virginia Tech; Senior Partner, Safety Performance Solutions

These are very practical books. I, myself, have been interested in the fundamental processes of human thinking. For creativity there is Lateral Thinking. For exploration there is the parallel thinking of the Six Thinking Hats. For perception there is the CoRT school programme. *The Exemplary Worker* series of books provide frameworks for focused thinking about specific situations. The frameworks guide the thinker to deal with the situation instead of messing about. That is why the books are so practical."

—**Dr. Edward de Bono**, Author of Lateral Thinking and Six Thinking Hats and creator of CoRT

The Exemplary Worker Book Series

EnviroThink™

to protect the environment

Gordon D. Shand

HDC Human Development Consultants Ltd.
PO Box 4710, Edmonton, AB, Canada T6E 5G5
www.hdc.ca
www.safethink.ca

EnviroThink™

Library and Archives Canada Cataloguing in Publication
Shand, Gordon D.
     EnviroThink to protect the environment / Gordon D. Shand.
(The exemplary worker book series)
ISBN 978-1-55338-056-6
     1. Business enterprises--Environmental aspects. 2. Environmental protection. 3. Critical thinking. 4. Environmental management. I. HDC Human Development Consultants II. Title. III. Series: Exemplary worker
HC79.E44S52 2014   363.7   C2014-902764-2

Published by HDC Human Development Consultants Ltd.

Published in Canada

HDC *Human Development Consultants Ltd.*

Website: www.hdc.ca
E-mail: hdc@hdc.ca
Phone: (780) 463-3909

Acknowledgements

Developing *The Exemplary Worker* book series has been challenging and rewarding. I am certainly grateful for all the help I have received to produce quality products. Over one hundred people have contributed to the quality of the content and presentation.

Generally, I developed the first draft of the books working on evenings and weekends. I would blitz the first draft for a book—I produced the draft in a month to three months. During those times, my family's gracious support allowed me to concentrate on the task and to dialogue with them about the concepts. Once a first draft was produced, consultants in my firm carried out several edits as time allowed. HDC's Production Department developed illustrations and formats to produce a book ready for validation by industry. Because the people from industry volunteered their time and some validations were conducted in sequence, the validation process for each book took up to six months or more.

Many staff contributed to the development process. I would like to acknowledge those consultants who struggled to gather relevant content when working with customers—they gave cause to identify the thinking strategies used by exemplary workers and to develop the training for HDC consultants. Many thanks to the consultants who worked so diligently with me to produce the books. They were adamant in adhering to our standards for quality, even when I was burned out and wanted to put closure to a topic. Thanks to Janelle Beblow, Art Deane, Alice Graham, Jean MacGregor, and Bruno Schoenfelder for the wonderful edits and feedback. Thanks to Phil Jenkins, Kris Vasey, and Denise Hodgins for developing the illustrations, formatting the documents, and creating the book covers. Thanks to Maria Peck for coordinating the validations and field tests and proofing text. Their personal support, commitment to quality, and attention to detail are greatly appreciated.

I have been exceptionally fortunate to work with so many wonderful people from industry. They have been great mentors—they have made many contributions to my personal growth. A special thanks to nearly a hundred people who have volunteered their time to validate and field test the strategies.

EnviroThink™

Who is *The Exemplary Worker* series for?

The Exemplary Worker series benefits:

- **Individuals** who want to have outstanding performance

- **Apprentices and students** who want to work safely and effectively

- **Supervisors** who want staff to be more effective

- **Trainers** who want to contribute to improved corporate, job, and employee performance
- **Trades and technology instructors** who want their apprentices and students to work safely and effectively

- **Instructional designers** who want to ensure that training is relevant, useful, and practical

- **HR managers** who want to improve the development and retention of exemplary workers

- **Operations staff** who want to optimize production and minimize losses

Contents

EnviroThink™

Table of Contents (continued)

Preface

In addition to being skilled, exemplary workers use a broad range of *critical thinking strategies* to maintain outstanding performance. Exemplary workers know what is important to their jobs and organizations—they put their efforts in the right places by doing the most important things, doing them effectively, and doing them efficiently. Because they know what is important to the job and the organization, they effectively coordinate their actions with others and make decisions in the best interest of their organizations. Knowledge and thinking skills empower workers to achieve exemplary performance, be flexible as workplaces continue to evolve, and provide leadership within the workplace.

Exemplary performance can have many benefits for you, the line worker, lead operator, foreman, or supervisor, including:
- increased job satisfaction
- being recognized by your peers and supervisors as an effective employee
- increased potential for keeping your job during slow economic times
- increased potential for receiving salary/wage increases or bonuses
- increased opportunity for new or different work assignments
- increased potential for promotion

Each of the seven books in *The Exemplary Worker* series focuses on one of five domains (**PEMEO**):
- **P**eople
- **E**quipment
- **M**aterials
- **E**nvironment
- **O**rganization

Loss and/or optimization (LO) are the main themes for the domains, creating the word **LO-PEMEO™**. LO-PEMEO stands for Loss and Optimization of People, Equipment, Materials, Environment, and Organization. As an example: **L**oss to **P**eople is illness and injury; **O**ptimizing **P**eoples' performance is working effectively and efficiently; **L**oss to **E**quipment is damage and shortened operating life; and **O**ptimizing **E**quipment is using equipment effectively and efficiently. The books place a strong emphasis on using **thinking strategies** and **asking quality questions**—the goals are to minimize losses and optimize performance of PEMEO.

The series of books addresses both loss and optimization of each domain. We recommend that you complete each of the first six books in the sequence. However, the books can be studied in any order without difficulty. The last book in the sequence, *MetaThink*, should be read last. *MetaThink* applies some of the thinking strategies addressed in previous books but in different ways and also addresses new thinking strategies useful for the workplace.

Introduction to *The Exemplary Worker* Series

Over the last twenty-five years, the process of discovering *what's important* for exemplary worker performance has gone full circle. The process began for me when I interviewed exemplary workers to identify relevant training content. My premise was that exemplary workers know what is important for people to do their jobs effectively. Over time, it became apparent to me that one of the reasons exemplary workers perform so well is that they use a set of generic thinking strategies. After starting a consulting firm to design and develop training, I developed a comprehensive internal training program for our consultants and technical writers who develop training programs. The training focused on using generic thinking strategies and critical questions to identify training content that helps workers perform effectively. With a lot of support, I have revised our consultant training program and made it available to the public for people to learn and refine their personal thinking strategies to be exemplary workers.

The Exemplary Worker books are presented as a series. The same concepts underlie all seven books. For example, a safety incident may cause harm to a person and result in other losses—work may be suspended, equipment and materials damaged, the environment harmed. The organization could also experience unpredicted costs and have its reputation harmed. This introduction provides a framework and the key concepts that apply to the series. The discovery process and happenstances that led to the development of *The Exemplary Worker* series are explained to provide a setting and context to give meaning to the underlying concepts.

The Discovery Process

For me, the real discovery process began in 1985 when I founded the consulting firm HDC Human Development Consultants Ltd. (HDC) to design and develop customized technical training programs. I believed that it was possible to develop quality training for any industry without having an in-depth understanding of the organization, its technology, or the tasks that its people perform. The premise was that a well-thought-out instructional design and development process combined with effective consulting skills would be sufficient.

As founder of the company, I felt that I was successful in providing leadership to identify training content important to my customers—customers often asked me to do additional work. If I could do the work well, then certainly others in the firm could as well and, for some deliverables, do better.

The Plan

The plan was that I would work with customers to develop the outline of the training program (curriculum) and identify critical content for the program. The training program would be documented in one of three ways:
- a list of specific courses
- a list of general training objectives
- a competency-based training profile

Competency-Based Training Profile

The following illustration is a *partial* example of a competency-based training profile. The profile is a visual presentation of the competencies (tasks and support knowledge) that specific work groups require to do their work safely and effectively.

ORIENTATION	Complete Company Orientation	Describe Roles and Responsibilities	Identify Local Structures and Facilities	Describe and Use Communication Systems	Identify Customers and their Expectations
SAFETY	Describe and Use Personal Safety Equipment	Review Safety Handbook	Complete First Aid Training	Decribe and Operate Personal Gas Monitors	Describe Codes of Practice
ENVIRONMENT	Describe Environmental Responsibilities	Describe and Store Hazardous Wastes	Describe and Monitor Gas Emissions	Take Waste Water Samples	Describe and Participate in Spill Response Exercises
GENERAL KNOWLEDGE AND SKILLS	Describe Flammable Gas Measurements	Use Portable Multi-Gas Monitor	Describe Reciprocating Compressors	Prepare Maintenance Requests	
ROUTINE TASKS	Carry out Routine Equipment Checks	Change Process Filters	Describe and Change Corrosion Coupons	Monitor and Adjust Inhibitor Injection	Perform Housekeeping
SITE-SPECIFIC KNOWLEDGE AND TASKS	Describe Remore Process	Start and Adjust Remore Process	Describe and Change Remore Output Parameters	Perform Emergency Shutdown of Remore Process	Shut down Remore Process for Maintenance

Critical content for each competency is a list of the key issues a buddy or supervisor would emphasize when coaching the trainee. The end product is a *scope document* listing the key issues and ensuring continuity between competencies—no overlaps or gaps in content. As an example of a scope document, here is a partial list of key issues for the competency *Purge Piping and Station Systems:*

- replacing one medium with another to prevent combustible or toxic condition
- important to prevent:
  - people being exposed to toxic gases
  - possibility of a fire
- piping should only be purged after system has been opened and exposed to a foreign substance
- stations purged in preparation for startup
- some stations have automatic purging for specific piping and equipment
- automatic purging sequence must be checked
- always purge in direction gas migrates (up or down)
- criteria for length of time to purge include volume, pressure, and amount of connected equipment

In a profiling workshop, I used a brainstorming technique with four to sixteen of the customer's employees to identify competencies and critical content. The workshops were mentally demanding. On the one hand, I was concerned that the scope of training and performance requirements be limited and only address competencies and content that were considered important to the workers, their supervisors, and the organization. On the other hand, I was concerned that critical issues affecting people and the business were not overlooked. During these workshop sessions, I was constantly searching for relevant, useful, and practical content. What do the workers do? Is there a special way of doing the task? How do they know they are doing a good job? What can go wrong? How can the equipment be damaged or its life shortened? What do you mean by product quality? What about safety and the environment? Does the organization have special policies and ways of doing business? What is important and to whom or what? What questions should I be asking the group? I did not have a clear set of criteria or a structured thinking process that I could use to provide leadership in identifying training content that was important to the worker and the supervisor.

Working with Subject Matter Experts (SMEs)

I certainly believed that asking quality questions was more important than providing content. Answers to the questions could be provided by the customer's experienced employees. The term *subject matter experts* (*SME*s) is often used to refer to the organization's staff who provide content to training consultants and technical writers. Unfortunately, some SMEs, having in-depth knowledge of the tasks, technology, and the organization, had difficulties identifying content important for training. These SMEs expected consultants to provide leadership to identify relevant content. I soon discovered that my consultants often had difficulties in providing leadership to SMEs trying to identify content that was relevant, practical, and useful. When reviewing the first draft of training modules, information that would help trainees do their jobs more effectively, efficiently, and safely would often be missing. Nor would the supervisor's concerns always be addressed. Sometimes, information would be included that was of little value in helping workers do their jobs well and making decisions in the best interest of their organizations. When consultants asked me for direction as to the types of content that were relevant for training, I could not provide a comprehensive explanation. If the company was going to be successful in the future, I needed to find ways to define content that was relevant, practical, and useful—content that contributed to employee, job, and corporate performance.

Customer feedback gave me reason to believe that I was providing adequate leadership to identify relevant content; that I was asking quality questions. The truth of the matter was I did not have a formal list of types of question I should ask. In many ways, I was relying on intuition to ask the right questions. I needed to find a way to articulate a content gathering strategy that consultants could use with a variety of customers in different lines of business, different technologies, different hiring practices and performance expectations, and different ways of conducting business. I needed to find a way to identify the specific types of question consultants could ask SMEs to identify important training content—content that would help workers perform their jobs safely and effectively and contribute to meeting corporate objectives.

To help our training consultants and technical writers gain a better understanding of our customers, their businesses, goals, and concerns, I took consultants along to the competency-based profiling sessions. Listening to the group discussions and individual insights about the work and the business always provided learning beyond the information recorded in the program outline and scope document. This learning should be valuable when working with SMEs to identify detailed content for the training resources. Having this preliminary knowledge about the customer seemed to help some consultants be better at identifying relevant training content, but other consultants continued to struggle. I concluded that knowledge about the customer was valuable but didn't give consultants the strategies they needed to provide leadership when working with SMEs.

The Importance of Training Content Being Relevant to the Organization, Job, and Employees

Project reviews with customers were very useful for gaining ideas on how to improve services and products. Feedback from SMEs was that HDC consultants asked more questions than anyone they had ever worked with before. On the other hand, our consultants felt that they didn't ask enough questions because relevant information had been missed. The real issue was to ask fewer questions but more *quality* questions—questions that addressed issues that were important to employees, the job, and the organization. Certainly, customers strongly indicated that identifying relevant, useful, and practical content was the most important quality concern they had regarding the development of training resources. Customers also were adamant that consultants provide direction and leadership when working with SMEs to identify relevant content.

At the close of each project, I would ask the customer what additional training might be useful for consultants to help them be more effective at identifying relevant content. Suggestions included that consultants could increase their technical knowledge, or have a better understanding about safety management systems, environment management systems, or management styles. In response to suggestions, we began providing additional internal training using off-the-shelf technical training materials when possible. The additional training helped consultants to better understand what SMEs were telling them but only resulted in marginal improvements in consultants being able to provide leadership to identify relevant content. I concluded that the knowledge is useful but not sufficient in helping consultants (and workers) to identify issues important to employee, job, and corporate performance.

To compound the problem of identifying relevant content, expectations in industry were changing from developing entry level training (do as I tell and show you and don't ask why) to exemplary level training (maximizing productivity and making quality decisions) and every level between those two extremes. These changing expectations created difficulties in determining the content and amount of detail to include in training and keeping within training development budgets. Customers were upset if training materials included content they did not want and were not willing to pay for. Customers could also be disappointed if the training did not include content that they considered important. In many ways, the concerns consultants had in understanding the customer's expectations are the same concerns an employee new to a job would have.

When I had worked with exemplary workers, I discovered that one of their strategies was to confirm expectations. So we used the same strategy and built more confirmation checks into the development process to ensure the content was what customers wanted. Unfortunately, the confirmation checks were good at confirming that the documented content was what customers wanted but did not effectively address concerns about omissions of content important to customers (e.g., safety, equipment life).

Identifying Thinking Strategies Used by Exemplary Workers

Developing internal training for consultants to effectively identify relevant, useful, and practical content proved to be very difficult. Having consultants participate in the profiling sessions to learn about the customer, developing scope documents, providing technical and organization training, and building in confirmation checks had some value but weren't sufficient in helping them to provide leadership to identify relevant training content.

The instructional systems design models I was familiar with generally placed a strong emphasis on instructional development processes and only provided marginal direction and strategies on how to provide leadership to identify content that was important to customers. Certainly, the design of instruction and the nature of the content had an effect on each other. I suspected that there were instructional designs in which generic module structures and generic types of content would work for some types of technology and associated training outcomes. It would be several more years, after we had a large inventory of customized self-instructional modules, before we were able to develop a set of generic boilerplates (list of section and sub-section titles) for specific technologies and training outcomes. These *boilerplates* provided general structures for self-instruction and listed the types of content that *could* be included (but not necessarily included) in each section. No doubt, the SMEs that I worked with had mentally created their own boilerplates to be effective when working with specific types of equipment.

My initial effort to develop training to identify relevant content proved to be fairly impractical. Fortunately, several events provided me with the fundamental concepts needed to develop strategies that consultants could use to identify relevant content.

One of HDC's customers had a very demanding supervisor who was exceptionally analytical. In fact, he was by far the most powerful analytical thinker I have met. He was also driven to prevent anything negative from happening. He would always be analyzing situations and wanted to know all the *hows* and *whys* about every aspect of the instructional design that came to mind. Once a week I would make a personal visit to address his concerns. On one of those visits, he demanded to know what type of content should be addressed in the training. He said he asked our consultant the same question and the consultant's response was that *he would write self-instruction on anything as long as we told him the content*. Obviously, the consultant was not providing leadership when working with the SME to identify training content that would help the operators perform their work safely and effectively. For me, it was confirmation that our internal training was not very effective in helping our consultants to provide leadership.

My immediate response to his demand was to give some general criteria for identifying relevant content. *Well, safety, environment, equipment life, product quality, and customer satisfaction are important. Adhering to legislation and making decisions are important, too.*

There was a long silence—a lot of mental processing was going on in his head. Finally, he nodded and said, *Good. Let's tell the consultant and the senior operator what you just said.* The bottom line for this customer was that the training we were developing would contribute to his staff doing their work effectively and safely and making good decisions.

The interaction I had with that customer was the moment of discovery for me! The three-hour drive back to the office gave me time to reflect on what had just happened. Obviously, until I was asked, I had not been able to see the forest for the trees. Ask any business person what is important to their business success and he or she would give a list of areas of concern similar to the one I gave to my customer. No doubt the business person's list would be more extensive and include additional concerns affecting productivity and controlling losses—all businesses want to get the most out of their assets, including their people. Businesses prefer to have exemplary workers, workers that contribute to business success. Certainly, the training we develop for customers must help workers be effective in doing their jobs.

Creating the LO-PEMEO Model to Identify Relevant Training

I reflected on the thinking process I was using to identify relevant content when developing training profiles and scope documents. The questions that I had been asking myself during the sessions addressed the optimization and prevention of losses primarily to People, Equipment, Materials, Environment, and the Organization as a whole. Surely, the questions would take on meaning when the work environment was considered. And one way of assessing the work environment was to consider the conditions, actions, and events within the workplace that affect PEMEO.

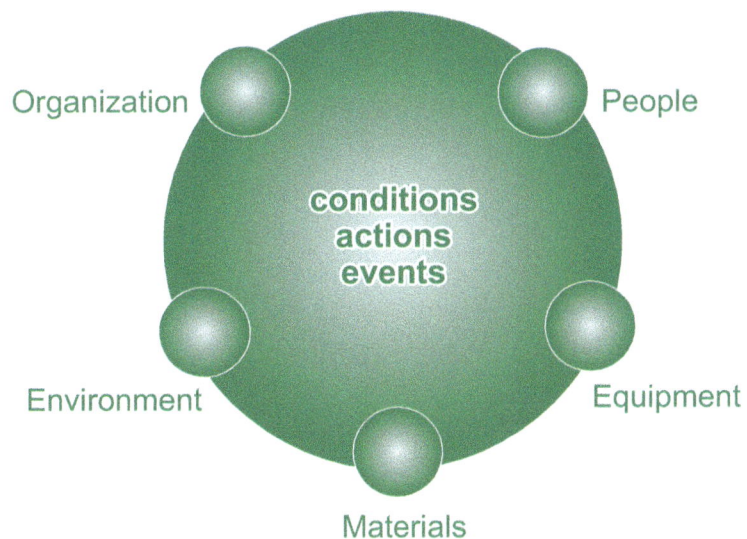

Most exciting for me, I could combine the concepts of optimization and controlling losses of organizational assets such as people and equipment to create a model and strategy for identifying relevant content. The LO-PEMEO model was born. Each of the five domains (people, equipment, materials, etc.) shown in the above illustration had potential for optimization and loss. An example of loss to people is illness and injury. Loss of materials when processing ore is the inefficient recovery of the desired products. Optimization of materials in construction is to use the right materials and maximize the use of the materials. The following illustration shows the combinations of loss and optimization of PEMEO.

LOSS					OPTIMIZATION	
Loss:	People	LP	P	OP	Optimization:	People
Loss:	Equipment	LE	E	OE	Optimization:	Equipment
Loss:	Materials	LM	M	OM	Optimization:	Materials
Loss:	Environment	LE	E	OE	Optimization:	Environment
Loss:	Organization	LO	O	OO	Optimization:	Organization

Exemplary workers consider the potential for Loss and Optimization of each domain of PEMEO (i.e., LO-PEMEO) while they work. So LO-PEMEO was used as the framework and structure for *The Exemplary Worker* series of books. For example, loss to people (LP) is safety—the book *SafeThink* focuses on using a structured critical thinking strategy to identify and predict hazardous situations to prevent illness and injury.

Interestingly, several years later, I was introduced to a loss control model created by Frank E. Bird that used PEME as an acronym. I have always wondered if it would have saved me a lot of effort if I had known of Bird's loss control model earlier. Or would that knowledge have put in place constraints such that I would never have created the LO-PEMEO model?

While driving back to my office, I thought about how fortunate I had been over the years to work with a lot of exemplary performers, many of them my SMEs. Our customers gave us SMEs who are exemplary workers because the belief is that exemplary workers know what is important for business success and will provide training content that is relevant to corporate, job, and employee performance. When I had asked the SMEs if there were any concerns about issues such as safety, equipment, or materials, they would often look at the ceiling and ponder for a while. If they said yes, they would go on and give me further clarification. If they said no, I would continue to ask different questions. When I thought about it, the questions that I asked SMEs usually focused on concerns about LO-PEMEO. I always wondered what the SMEs were thinking when they were looking at the ceiling and pondering the answers to my questions. Eventually, I asked them. Interestingly, different SMEs from different companies and lines of business had similar concerns. For example, damage to equipment often involved shock from a sudden change in physical forces or temperature. The sources for causing damage could be people, material, or any of the other three domains. In fact, *each domain has the potential to affect the other domains.* Whether the SMEs were aware of it or not, they were mentally searching for specific workplace concerns relating to LO-PEMEO. In many ways, even at the detailed level, *the thinking strategies of exemplary workers were similar and generic.* Certainly, being aware of one's own thinking strategies contributes to planning and working effectively and helps to communicate effectively when collaborating with others and mentoring apprentices.

Linking Corporate, Job, and Employee Performance

When organizations develop standards, procedures, and training, they want to realize an improvement in corporate performance. Improving *corporate performance* is often achieved by either filling a gap in performance or by preparing the organization to move towards new goals. The following illustration lists some criteria that can be used to measure corporate performance.

PERFORMANCE REPORT

Customer Satisfaction	UP
Production	UP
Product Quality	UP
Equipment Run Time	UP
Equipment Damage	DOWN
Energy Consumption	DOWN
Material Waste	DOWN
Personal Injuries	DOWN
Maintenance Costs	DOWN
Environment Damage	DOWN
Rework Time	DOWN

At the operational or job level, the supervisor also has concerns about performance. Within his or her roles, responsibilities, and authority, the supervisor is expected to maximize productivity and minimize losses. Improved *job performance* contributes to improved corporate performance. The supervisor therefore represents the concerns and goals of the organization and must use specific resources and assets (including people) to effectively achieve the goals. The supervisor must also be able to motivate, coordinate, and assign staff to effectively carry out the work. Furthermore, worker performance affects job performance which, in turn, affects corporate performance.

Employee performance affects business results. Employees are expected to work effectively and efficiently and make good use of materials and technology. Expectations of performance are articulated to line employees both orally and in writing. In turn, employees have concerns about understanding the expectations and working safely, effectively, and efficiently to meet the expectations. The following illustration is of a person new to a job asking questions relating to corporate, job, and employee performance issues.

What's important to the business?

What does the team leader expect of me?

What am I supposed to do?

How am I supposed to do it?

How do I know I've done well?

How does my work affect others?

Is there a better way?

What tools and equipment are used?

Could I get hurt?

Could I injure others?

Could I damage the equipment?

Does this product affect the environment?

How much waste is acceptable?

How can I prevent...?

Will the customer be satisfied?

What should I do if ...?

What would happen if ...?

Do I have the authority to take action?

What action?

Whom should I inform?

What does ...?

How does ...?

What caused ...?

What is the reason?

What are the consequences for ...?

What questions should I be asking?

What answers do I need?

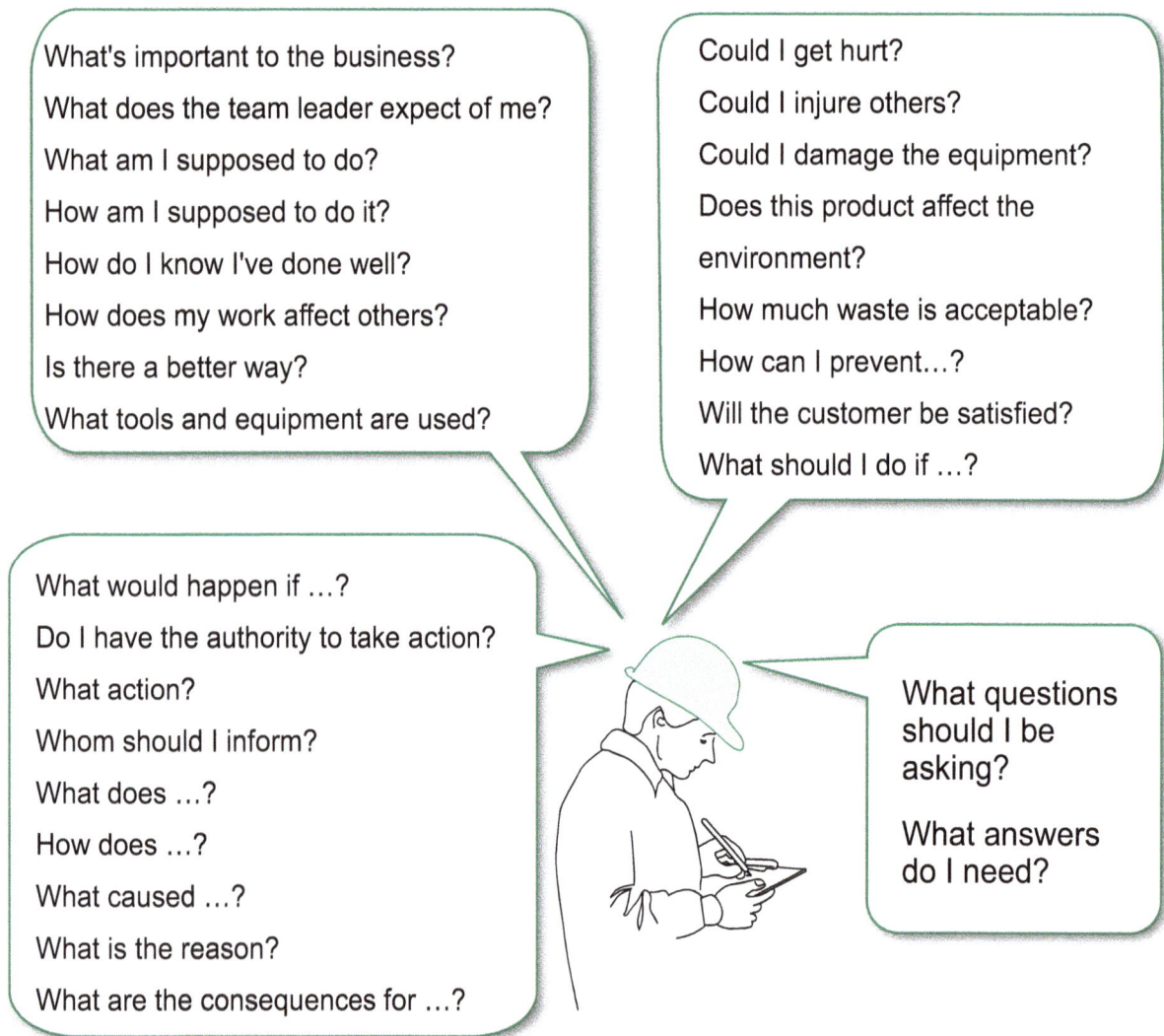

Many of the questions are generated by the LO-PEMEO strategy and focus on performance:

- What is important?
- What are the issues?
- What questions should I ask?

The person new to the job needs answers to the questions in the illustration to quickly learn to do that job effectively and efficiently. Interestingly, two employees with similar experiences and skills who are new to a job can perform quite differently. One employee will be uncertain about the work and become stressed if work conditions change. The other employee will initiate actions and make good work-related decisions for the organization within a few weeks. One of the factors that makes the difference in performance between the two employees is the knowledge about what is important to job and corporate performance. Understanding *what is important* provides criteria for focusing one's efforts and for making decisions. LO-PEMEO is a good start in identifying what is important to the organization. Although many of the issues identified by LO-PEMEO are generic, each organization has its own business strategies, resources, and priorities. As such, each organization could place a different emphasis on each issue identified by LO-PEMEO. And that's why asking the *right* questions is so valuable. Questions focus on key issues; the answers to the questions are unique to the organization, workplace, and specific circumstances. *The Exemplary Worker* series provides many of the questions that workers need to ask of themselves and of others to achieve exemplary performance.

Understanding Organizations for Exemplary Worker Performance

Exemplary workers understand what is important to the organization so that they put their efforts in the right places, do the right things, and make good decisions in the best interests of their organizations. For workers to have exemplary performance, they need to have an understanding of organizations in general, and a specific understanding of their own organization. Training and performance consultants also need to have a general understanding of organizations to be effective at developing customized training—training that is relevant, useful, practical, and reflects the organization for what it is. There is a lot of literature on organizations but most of it is more complex than training consultants need. Generally, the literature does not directly address issues important to designing and developing customized training for industry.

So, what issues are important? For consultants at HDC (and exemplary workers in other organizations) to be effective, they must be able to identify and understand organizational issues from different points of view. Imagine a roomful of statues facing in different directions. The room has many doors, each opened by a different work group or discipline. Each doorway has a different view of the statues.

For consultants to get a broader understanding of the organization, they need to view the statues from different doors. Ideally, consultants would walk around the statues to get many different points of view. The consultant must be prepared to consider different points of view within a specific organization to be effective at understanding the organization and identifying issues important to employee, job, and corporate performance.

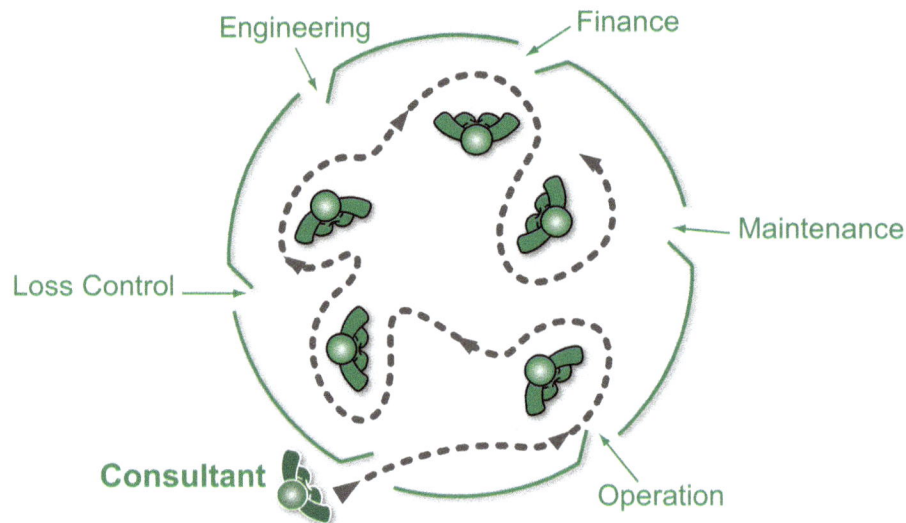

Both exemplary workers and training/performance consultants benefit from an understanding of relationships between business resources, organizational structure, business strategies, corporate objectives, and performance standards. Exemplary workers gain an understanding as to how their line of work fits into the organization as a whole. In doing so, they appreciate how their work affects others and they potentially make better use of organizational resources. This understanding about organizations also helps training consultants and technical writers to be more effective at designing and developing training that is customized, reflects the business, and has excellent value for the customer.

The approach I take with consultants to learn about organizations is to pretend to build a new business. Would the line of business be a service or a product? What is the mission? If the business is a service, then performing tasks is the main way to generate revenue and tools/equipment provide support for carrying out the work. If the line of business is to use technology to make products, then the technology dictates many of the tasks that workers must do. Having resources to achieve specific results is essential but not sufficient for business success. The resources must also be managed effectively. The following illustration identifies some key constituents of a business.

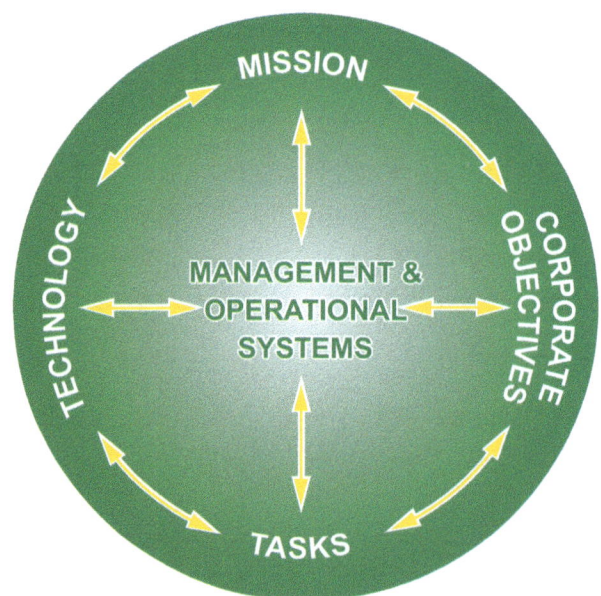

The book *JobThink* uses the previous model to provide a practical way for workers to understand organizations. This understanding helps workers to effectively focus their efforts and make decisions in the best interests of their organizations.

Of particular interest are the *corporate objectives*. Corporate objectives provide direction for using technology, performing tasks, and coordinating work to effectively achieve the corporate mission. The following table lists areas of concern, common to many organizations, for which corporate objectives may be developed.

Areas addressed by Corporate Objectives

• safety	• quality	• public image
• environment	• waste control	• public disruption
• legislation	• loss control	• reputation
• equipment reliability and life	• cost control	• communication
• equipment optimization	• customer satisfaction	• teamwork
• energy use		

For a specific organization, a list of corporate objectives can be generated by expanding the organization's strategic business objectives or by using LO-PEMEO. Some companies issue strategic business objectives to provide direction to employees as to where to put their energy and focus for business success. Strategic business objectives identify what the organization must do well to be successful. For example, leaders in an organization may believe that it is essential for business success to have reliable service and satisfied customers. Organizations may identify five to eight strategic objectives. Within a department, the list of objectives (or goals) may be expanded in more detail to address issues specific to the department's mandate.

The expanded list of corporate objectives can also be generated using LO-PEMEO— each of the items in the above table relates to one or more of the LO-PEMEO domains.

Corporate objectives are fundamental to exemplary performance because they define what is *important* to the organization, the job, and workers. Corporate objectives provide a **formal link** between organizational goals and worker performance. Workers can use corporate objectives as criteria for working effectively and efficiently and for making decisions in the best interest of their organizations. Training consultants and technical writers can use corporate objectives to identify relevant, useful, and practical training content. Refer to my book, *Interviewing to Gather Relevant Content for Training* for:
- information about applying critical thinking skills to identify relevant content for training
- an interviewing process that consultants and technical writers can use to interview SMEs to gather relevant content

EnviroThink™

Developing Training to Identify What is Important to Employee, Job, and Corporate Performance

With the LO-PEMEO and business models, I could now develop training for consultants to provide leadership to identify relevant content. The LO-PEMEO model was the most practical approach to use to structure the training because it relates directly to work and job issues. The organizational model can be integrated into the training on loss and optimization of organization, LO-O. For the training on these models to be useful, the training needs to be flexible and apply to a broad range of work, technology, and organizations. The training must also provide strategies for people to think through their work. That is what exemplary workers do—they think through their work. And, the thinking processes are generic so they apply to all types of industries, work environments, and jobs.

All of the training to identify relevant content is founded on using thinking strategies. An emphasis is placed on *concepts* and *generalities* to maintain a broad application of the thinking strategies. Furthermore, the thinking involves asking questions relating to LO-PEMEO. Asking questions is important to maintaining the broad application of the thinking strategies and helping people remain mentally engaged. Asking the *right* questions is often more important than finding the answers, because if the right questions are asked, answers can usually be found— answers that contribute to exemplary employee, job, and corporate performance.

Over several years, I developed training for all the combinations of LO-PEMEO. I also expanded the training to include consulting processes and a performance and training model to design, develop, and implement competency-based training and performance management systems. I was very fortunate to have excellent support from staff to edit and refine the training. HDC staff made important contributions to the training content and presentation. And, after the training resources were in use, we refined them further.

Developing *The Exemplary Worker* Series

After the HDC consultants' training resources had been used for ten years, I decided to go full circle and modify the resources for general use. A major rewrite was required; the new audience was very broad and the lines of work very diverse. The instructional design content had to be deleted. New and different examples of applying the thinking strategies were required for the books. To help the reader, each book required new learning activities. Exemplary workers in industry needed to field test and validate the content. Staff also needed to make major contributions to ensure the quality of each book. It took over six thousand hours to develop *The Exemplary Worker* series. In addition, industry has volunteered more than a thousand hours to field test and validate the content.

The Exemplary Worker series has many suggestions to help you not only be aware of your own thinking strategies but also help you to refine your strategies to achieve exemplary performance. You will also be better at mentoring others to perform better.

Gordon D. Shand
Edmonton, Alberta
Canada

Glossary

Autoclaving	using a container of superheated steam to sterilize
Air emissions	material released to the air that may or may not have significant environmental impact because of its physical, chemical, or biological nature, or may be treated to minimize environmental impact
Biohazardous	biological agent that can harm living things
Bioremediation	a treating process that uses micro-organisms to change hazardous materials and waste into less toxic materials
Carbon footprint	carbon dioxide and other carbon-based gases discharged in the environment by specific human, industrial, and natural activities
Contaminant	any material, odor, sound, vibration, heat, or radiation that can cause harm to the natural environment or human health
Cyclone filters	equipment that swirls a gas or liquid to separate out solid particles
Ecosystem	a community of living things and its physical and chemical environment
Effluent	liquid materials in solution (as well as some solids) released into a body of water. Effluents may or may not have significant environmental impact because of their physical, chemical, or biological nature, or may be treated to minimize environmental impact.
Electrostatic precipitator	equipment that uses a high-voltage electrical charge to remove dust from air
Environment	air, water, and land, including all living things
Fugitive emissions	escape of emissions into the environment from equipment and piping
Hazardous waste	materials which may affect the health of living organisms or cause damage to the environment if they are released directly to the environment
Leaching	extraction of soluble materials caused by water filtering down through the soil or wastes
Mitigate	to make less severe

EnviroThink™

Pollutant	material that interferes with the natural functioning of an ecosystem. Pollutants may be biodegradable or non-degradable.
Pollution	contamination of the environment with substances or energy that interfere with human health, the quality of life, or the natural functioning of an ecosystem
Potability	the characteristics of water that make it drinkable
Reclamation	process of modifying a site for a different use (e.g., wetlands to agricultural use; industrial use to parkland). Reclamation activities generally need approval and, depending on the site, may include:

- removing installations, buildings, and roadways
- remediating soil and/or groundwater
- changing site drainage and/or topography
- adding topsoil and planting vegetation

Remediation	process of reducing contaminant concentrations in soil or groundwater to levels specified for the site's current or intended use (e.g., reducing lead concentrations in soil slated for residential use). Depending on the site, remediation methods may include:

- soil removal/replacement
- soil treatment (using heat, chemicals, or micro-organisms that convert contaminants to less harmful substances)
- installing barriers, liners, or capping materials to immobilize or contain contaminants (e.g., to prevent downward migration to groundwater)

Sustainable development	carry out business activities in a way that maintains the ecology. A broader definition includes the interdependent sustainability of cultural diversity, the economy, and the environment.
Turbidity	a measure of the cloudiness of water
Waste	materials which can no longer be used for their original purpose and require treatment or disposal

NOTE

Environmental protection is a relatively new field of study and the terminology is still evolving. Terms such as *hazardous waste*, *pollutant*, and *remediate* are defined to suit the purpose of the user (individual, organization, or regulatory jurisdiction). Many terms have more than one definition; the definitions may be general (broad) or very precise.

In this book, environmental terms are used generally so that the learning focuses on environmental concepts and the thinking strategy. Learners who need a more precise definition of a particular term should contact an environmental specialist in their organization or regulatory jurisdiction.

Training Objectives

Upon completion of this book, you will be able to:

- Define environmental terms
- Describe the three components under which environmental issues can be defined
- List three types of actions which can have an impact on three environmental components
- Describe the purpose of environmental risk assessments
- Describe organizational activities to protect the environment
- Describe elements of an environmental management system
- List the reasons organizations protect the environment
- Identify strategies that can be used at the job level to protect the environment
- Describe the critical thinking strategy to protect the environment
- Apply the environmental critical thinking strategy to your organization and job

Introduction

This book is one of *The Exemplary Worker* series of books. Books in the series all focus on using critical thinking strategies to identify **what is important** to employees, the job, and the organization. Each book focuses on one of five domains (**PEMEO**):

P People

E Equipment

M Materials

E Environment

O Organization

Within each book, loss and/or optimization (LO) are the main themes, hence the word LO-PEMEO™:

Themes	Books
L-P Loss to People (Safety)	*SafeThink* Use a structured thinking strategy to identify and predict hazardous situations.
O-P Optimize People's Performance	*WorkThink* Work effectively and efficiently.
LO-E Loss and Optimization of Equipment	*EquipThink* Use tools and equipment effectively and efficiently.
LO-M Loss and Optimization of Materials	*MatThink* Use materials effectively and efficiently.
LO-E Loss and Optimization of the Environment	*EnviroThink* Protect the environment.
LO-O Loss and Optimization of the Organization	*JobThink* Contribute to job and corporate performance.
LO-PEMEO Use thinking strategies for the workplace	*MetaThink* Integrate thinking strategies for exemplary performance.

The fundamental premise of LO-PEMEO is to *ask questions*. By asking yourself questions, you remain alert. By seeking answers, you continually learn and become more effective in the workplace and adaptable to changes. The big question is: *What questions should I ask?* The questions identified in LO-PEMEO help you to ask many of the right questions to do your job effectively and efficiently with minimal effort.

As the natural environment becomes less and less able to sustain itself, people are becoming more aware of the need to maintain the diversity of life, sustain renewable resources, and protect human and environmental health. In response

to these concerns, people are putting more effort into
conducting business in a way that protects the environment.
Many organizations have implemented a comprehensive
environmental management system to effectively manage
the complex environmental aspects of their businesses and
achieve their environmental protection goals.

There is often a trade-off between protecting the natural
environment and providing jobs, goods, and services.
Conducting business in a way that protects the environment
often requires a significant investment.

Different organizations have different types of impact on the
environment. The specific makeup of their environmental
impact programs depends on the potential risks to the
environment and the public. To do business, organizations
may need to carry out a variety of environmental protection
activities:
- conduct environmental impact studies as part of the
  planning stage, during the design of facilities, and after
  operations start
- design facilities to treat, control, and monitor the release of
  substances that could be harmful to the environment
- implement specific methods to store and transport wastes
- establish emergency response plans and respond to
  incidents to minimize the impact on the environment
- carry out reclamation activities to restore the environment
  to its original state after operations are complete

Organizations and employees are guided in the activities to
protect the environment by:
- legislation enacted by federal, provincial/state, and regional
  governments
- standards established by environmental agencies and
  industry associations
- social responsibilities of groups and individuals

As part of a company's efforts to protect the environment,
individual employees have important roles and
responsibilities. Employees often identify and carry out the
first response to environmental issues. Their ability and

commitment to protecting the environment is important to achieving the organization's environmental goals.

This book focuses on using a *critical thinking strategy* to identify and respond to environmental issues in the workplace. The advantages of this strategy are that it:

- can be applied to any job position
- can be applied before, during, and after a task or job has been completed
- provides a means for you to think about the impact your work has on the environment (whether or not there are documented practices and procedures)
- provides a means for you to be better prepared to act if conditions develop that could have an impact on the environment

This critical thinking strategy involves asking yourself specific questions relating to environmental issues:

Environmental Issues
1   Impact on the natural environment
2. Pollutant release rates
3. Measuring and monitoring pollutant releases
4. Controlling the impact on the environment
5. Safe disposal of wastes
6. Protecting the environment when there are technical problems
7. Minimizing environmental impact when there are emergencies
8. Keeping informed about organizational activities affecting the environment
9. Restoring the environment to its intended use
10. Conserving energy
11. Minimizing material consumption

This strategy applies to both technical and work processes. Technical processes usually involve starting, monitoring, adjusting, and shutting down production systems. Work processes usually involve using tools and equipment to carry out a task or do a job.

This book describes in detail the critical thinking strategy to protect the environment. Each environmental issue is described individually with specific examples. Learning activities give you the opportunity to determine how each environmental issue applies to your job.

Try this:
1. Give examples of how your company impacts the environment.
_____
_____
_____
_____

(continued)

Try this:

2. Give examples of how you could adjust the way you work to reduce the impact on the environment.

    _____

    _____

    _____

    _____

3. Give examples of how your company could reduce its impact on the environment.

    _____

    _____

    _____

    _____

Section 2

Environmental Concepts

2.1 The Natural Environment

The natural environment may be defined as the air, water, and land upon which life depends. An ecosystem includes living and non-living components: air, water, or land, natural processes such as weather, and living organisms. For example, deserts and swamps are ecosystems.

EnviroThink™

Ecosystem:
a community of living things and its physical and chemical environment

An ecosystem will remain balanced if there are no changes to the environment. In a balanced ecosystem, species maintain relatively stable populations and remain largely unchanged. A change in one part of an ecosystem may cause a ripple of changes throughout the ecosystem as well as through other ecosystems. Some species may flourish while others become extinct.

Changes to ecosystems can be initiated by natural processes such as changes in weather or by the activities of any living organism. The introduction of new species, such as plants, animals, and insects, can cause major changes because the new species may not have natural enemies. The result can be overpopulation which may consume resources used by other species, choking them out, or directly harming them.

Pollutant:
material that interferes with the natural functioning of an ecosystem

Changes to ecosystems can also be initiated by human activities that remove, modify, or add to air, water, or land. One of the more obvious human activities is adding pollutants. The environment will be harmed if the quantity of pollutants is more than the environment can handle without experiencing change. For example, small quantities of sewage can be released to a river without causing harm because the river's ecosystem is resilient and assimilates the sewage. However, as the quantity of sewage released to the river increases, the river's ecosystem becomes threatened.

2.2 Human Impact on the Natural Environment

Many human activities have either a positive or a negative effect on the environment. These environmental issues can be classified according to their impact on the quality of air, quality of water, and quality of land. In some cases, an activity that affects one category also affects other categories. For example, pollutants released to the atmosphere can drift over large areas or long distances. Through precipitation, the pollutants can contaminate surface water and land, causing harm to aquatic life, plants, and animals as well as humans. The *quality* of air, water, and land is of primary concern.

A change in air, water, or land quality has the potential to affect the health and survival of all living organisms, including humans.

Examples of changes affecting the quality of air, water, and land are:
- the quality of fresh air can be affected by increases in ozone and particulates
- the quality of land can be affected by tailings from mines, permanently removing trees, and clearing land for agriculture

- the quality of water can be affected by controlling the flow rates of rivers and by discharging pollutants into the water.

Any activity that removes, modifies, or adds to air, water, or land can have an impact on the natural environment. The following table shows the relationship of the three types of activities and the three components of the environment.

Action	Environmental Component		
	Air	Water	Land
Remove	effect on quality	effect on quality	effect on quality
Modify	effect on quality	effect on quality	effect on quality
Add	effect on quality	effect on quality	effect on quality

Because the natural environment is very complex, defining quality and determining the impact of activities on the environment can be difficult. Other sections of this book provide a more in depth explanation about air, water, and land quality. Examples are also provided on how various activities that remove, modify, or add to the environment can affect the quality of air, water, and land.

This book focuses on a critical thinking strategy that involves asking specific questions relating to specific environmental issues. All of the critical thinking questions addressed in this book directly or indirectly relate to controlling, preventing, or responding to activities and incidents that affect the quality of air, water, and land.

2.3 Environmental Standards

Environmental standards are targets or goals for governments, organizations, and individuals to meet in order to protect the natural environment. Environmental standards may also change in response to research.

Standards established by governments, various agencies, and organizations themselves minimize damage by:
- controlling the use of natural resources
- minimizing the environmental impact caused by industrial activities

In addition to legislation, various agencies such as the United Nations, International Organization for Standards (ISO), and industrial associations establish environmental standards, practices, and guidelines.

Refer to the Appendix for more information about organizations that establish, support, and enforce environmental standards.

Check your knowledge

1. The word *ecosystem* can be defined as _____.
    a. the relationship of plants and insects
    b. a community of living things and its physical and chemical environment
    c. the way a community of species interacts
    d. the population, age, gender, and health of a related set of living organisms

2. The word *pollutant* can be defined as _____.
    a. anything that is released to air, water, or land
    b. material that is released to the air that has an odor
    c. anything released to the environment that shouldn't be there
    d. material that interferes with the natural functioning of an ecosystem

3. Any action that removes, modifies, or adds to the environment may have an impact on the environment.
    a. true
    b. false

Answers

1. b   2. d   3. a

(continued)

Check your knowledge

Try this:

1. List one major source of air pollution.

   _____

2. Give an example where human activity has changed the landscape.

   _____

3. List one major source of water pollution.

   _____

Environmental Management Strategies

Governments, the public, special interest groups, and organizations are interested in protecting the natural environment. The goal is to sustain business activities in a way that protects, enhances, and makes wise use of the environment. When an organization proposes a new facility, the organization may have to conduct an environmental risk assessment (environmental impact assessment) to obtain approval to build. The purpose of an assessment is to determine the risks of causing harm to the environment so that decisions can be made regarding business initiatives. For example, based on an assessment, it may be decided that:

- the trade-off of environmental risk versus socioeconomic benefit may be acceptable and the business proposal accepted
- specific risk issues are of concern and adjustments to business facilities, processes, products, or services may have to be made to reduce risk
- the project gets rejected because it has an unacceptable level of risk of harming the environment

This section describes:
- environmental risk assessment
- organizational activities to protect the environment
- elements of an environmental management system

3.1 Environmental Risk Assessment

Environmental Risk Assessments (ERAs) can be very comprehensive, complex, and costly. A broad range of interested stakeholders and disciplines may participate in an ERA, including:
- risk assessment specialists
- scientists from various disciplines (e.g., toxicology)
- engineers
- safety and health specialists
- management
- operators and maintenance staff
- the public

Although various risk assessment methods can be used, all risk assessments are based on the concept of cause and effect.

level of risk = *probability* of an event (cause) occurring and *severity* of consequences (effect)

The level of risk increases with an increase in probability and/or severity. Given specific risk information, stakeholders must make decisions about the issues. An important factor affecting the outcomes of the decision-making process is the stakeholders' tolerance for risk. Some people are willing to take risks; others are not. The decisions made by stakeholders who have a high tolerance for risk may be different from the decisions made by those with a low risk tolerance.

Regardless of the tolerance level for risk of the stakeholders, to make informed decisions, they need quality information about:
- the potential of harming the environment
- the effects the events may have on the environment

To understand the specific relationships between causes and effects, the particular circumstances must be understood:
- The business and its surroundings must be described.
- The business location, technology, activities, processes, products, and services need to be examined.
- The business surroundings, including both natural and human environments, need to be documented.
- The presence of lakes, streams, and land features need to be noted.
- Population counts of various aquatic and land species may need to be carried out. Specific species may be examined to determine age, size, and health. This information may be used as benchmarks for future reference.

Identifying Potential Causes

Identifying the potential causes of harm to the environment can include examining:
- the physical location of the facility, including access roads and material storage (e.g., changing watershed, changing migration routes, changing aesthetics)
- continuing business activities (e.g., release of materials and energy to the air, water, and land, increased noise caused by local activity and transportation, odors, use of renewable and non-renewable natural resources)

- unpredicted incidents (e.g., equipment failure, leaks, spills, fires)

The **physical location** of a facility may be of concern to the public. If the facility is part of or close to populated areas, traffic patterns can change and there may be a potential increase in risk to human health. The facility may contribute to or take away from the beauty of the area. In some cases, the physical location of a facility may make economic sense but pose an increased risk to an environmentally sensitive area. Some segments of the population may wish to have the area used for something else, such as a park.

Business activities can involve the release of waste materials to the air, water, and land. Hazardous materials may be stored on site or transported from or to other locations. The types and quantities of hazardous materials must be determined. Noise and odors must be considered because they can affect both natural and human environments.

Unpredicted incidents that result in leaks, spills, and uncontrolled releases of materials to the environment may be of concern. A variety of risk assessment methods can be used to identify potential hazardous incidents—the events, causes, and effects:

- Hazard and Operability Study (HAZOP)
- Failure Mode and Effects Analysis (FMEA)
- Fault Tree Analysis (FTA)
- Critical Task Analysis

Each of these methods requires specialized personnel to conduct a detailed analysis of the technology, processes, practices, and procedures. To determine potential incidents, a *what if* approach is often taken regarding equipment condition, operating parameters, material specifications, and task performance. For example:

- *What if a container of hazardous product falls off a truck?*
- *What if the pressure in a vessel is greater than the vessel's design limits?*
- *What if a specific component fails?*
- *What if a person fails to close a specific valve?*
- *What if a fire occurs?*

The probability (chance, likelihood) of such events occurring must also be considered. Risk increases with an increase in probability.

Determining Potential Consequences

Consequences (the effects and the severity of the effects) must be determined after the potential causes of harm to the environment and the probability of an incident occurring have been identified. Consequences can be far reaching, not only having implications for the natural environment, but also posing risks to other aspects of an organization. Such risks include health and safety of employees and the public as well as financial and production risks.

Determining the consequences for the natural environment can be very difficult. Often there is a degree of uncertainty because of the large number of factors that must be taken into account, including:

- the complexity of the interrelationships of living components and their relationships with the non-living environment

- the amount of agent (e.g., noise, chemical) and duration of exposure that specific organisms or species can tolerate without being harmed
- the effect that two or more agents have on the environment. Some chemicals may cause more harm when found together than the harm caused individually. In other cases, the chemicals may counteract each other. For example, an acid and base could potentially neutralize each other, reducing the harm that each chemical could cause to the environment.
- the effect of changes to the food chain. Changes to the population of a species or the addition or depletion of a species can affect other species.
- the time it takes for an agent to cause harm to the environment
- long-term effects on the environment. The environment may or may not recover over a long period of time.

A variety of specialists may be required to determine the environmental impacts. They may study a variety of living things, including micro-organisms, plants, and animals that live in water and on land. The toxic effects of various chemicals may have to be researched. Impacts may be reported in mathematical terms. For example, for a given amount and duration of exposure, the potential of a chemical to cause cancer is one in 500,000. The amount of uncertainty as to the predicted impacts may also be stated.

To help decision makers, risk to the environment may be reported as worst-case and best-case scenarios. Risk to human health and safety and financial losses may also be considered. If they feel that the assessment is not adequate for making an informed decision, additional assessments may be done. If the decision makers determine that the risks are too high, the proposal may be rejected or recommendations may be made to reduce risk. Depending on the circumstances, risk can be reduced in many ways, for example:

- use different raw materials
- reduce waste production or find uses for the waste
- make technical changes to reduce the potential of failures
- improve monitoring and controls of processes
- improve fire detection and suppression
- use different product containment
- erect berms and dykes to reduce noise or contain spills
- develop contingency plans to respond to incidents

The changes may be accepted by the organization or the project may be abandoned if the protective measures are considered too costly or ineffective.

The environmental risk assessment described previously focuses primarily on facilities, processes, products, and services. A different strategy, *Life Cycle Assessment*, could also be used.

This strategy is concerned with the cradle-to-grave impact of a product. In addition to assessing the business facility and activities, the use of raw materials, product use, and product disposal must also be considered. This type of assessment not only increases the potential for improved environmental protection, but can also provide specific business benefits for organizations. Less costly materials may be identified or less hazardous materials might be employed, reducing the purchase and disposal costs to consumers. Both initiatives could improve the manufacturer's competitive advantage.

Environmental issues and regulations can be very complex. Many organizations find it necessary to take a systems approach to effectively manage the complex environmental aspects of their business and achieve their environmental goals. The answers to the eleven environmental issues listed in the introduction to this book may form the framework for developing an effective environmental management system.

Check your knowledge

1. When organizations apply for approval to build new facilities, government legislation may require them to assess and evaluate the environmental risks within their organization.
   a. true
   b. false

2. The purpose of an environmental risk assessment is to _____.
   a. assess the health of all organisms and species to determine which ones are in danger of extinction
   b. determine the risk that industrial activities might have on harming the natural environment
   c. determine the risk of specific plants becoming overabundant and choking out other plants
   d. determine the amount of cross-breeding of genetically altered plants and animals

(continued)

Check your knowledge

Answers

1. a   2. b

Try this:

1. List one major source of air pollution.

    _____

2. Give an example where human activity has changed the landscape.

    _____

    _____

3. List one major source of water pollution.

    _____

    _____

4. The risk of an organization potentially harming the environment varies according to its type of business activities. On a scale of 1 to 5, where 1 is low and 5 is high, rate your organization for risk of potentially harming the environment and give the reasons for your rating.

    _____

    _____

    _____

    _____

    _____

3.2 Organizational Activities to Protect the Environment

Organizations may carry out a variety of activities to protect the environment. The following information provides a brief description of some of those environmental management strategies.

Establish pollutant release rates—Operational licenses and environmental permits may state the limits and standards for releases. Releases may be based on:
- total allowable quantities that can be discharged
- time-weighted allowable concentrations
- emission rates

Effluent:
liquid materials in solution (as well as some solids) released into a body of water

Monitoring and measuring discharge rates—Regulations may require the organization to use monitoring equipment to identify the quantity and type of material being released to the air, water, and land. Discharge rates of air emissions and effluents can be continuously monitored or sampled on a regular basis. Legislation requires that test results be documented and reported to a government agency.

Environmental impact assessments—Depending on the circumstances, a variety of methods can be used to measure the impact that business activities have on the environment. These methods include:
- continuously collecting airborne pollutants at various distances from a facility's perimeter to determine the types and quantities of pollutants affecting the land
- taking water samples from lakes and rivers at various depths to determine the amount of contaminants present
- taking water samples from test wells drilled to the depth of the water table to test for groundwater contamination
- taking soil samples
- conducting impact studies and surveys to determine the population, distribution, and health of various species of plants, animals, birds, and fish. Sometimes blood samples are taken or a representative sample of a species is examined to determine the types and quantities of absorbed toxins.
- monitoring noise

Legislation requires that test results be documented and reported to a government agency. If there are concerns that the environment is being harmed, additional tests may be performed to help decision makers determine the best course of action.

Controls to limit environmental impact—Technology can be used to minimize the release of pollutants in the form of gas, liquid, dust, or solid. Industrial processes may be adjusted to keep the quantity of pollutants generated to a minimum.

Storage and disposal of wastes—Hazardous wastes are materials that may affect the health of living organisms or cause damage to the environment. Government regulations may specify the quantities and methods for storing hazardous waste on-site.

Government regulations specify methods to treat hazardous, non-hazardous, and unclassified wastes to reduce their impact on the environment. Specific methods for disposal may have to be used.

Transportation of Dangerous Goods (TDG) regulations specify the methods that must be used to transport hazardous wastes to disposal sites.

Contingencies for dealing with process upsets and equipment failure—Organizations often develop and document policies, practices, and procedures for normal business activities to optimize the use of assets and minimize the risk of incurring losses. For instance, routine maintenance of equipment may be carried out to minimize failure. However, should process upsets and equipment failures occur, specific plans may be in place to minimize the impact on the environment. Some examples include:

- Emissions and effluents containing excess pollutants may be reprocessed, diverted to storage tanks, or burnt.
- Containment dykes may be used to contain leaks or spills.
- Specific policies, practices, and procedures may be established to deal with upsets, abnormal operations, and equipment failure.
- Employees may receive training to act effectively under normal and abnormal operating and maintenance conditions.

Emergency response—Organizations may develop comprehensive emergency response programs that include:

- doing risk assessments
- taking preventative measures
- providing emergency response equipment
- providing employee training
- coordinating emergency responses with outside agencies such as fire departments, hospitals, and police
- preparing emergency response assistance plans for the transportation of dangerous goods

Should an incident occur, the organization often carries out an incident investigation to determine the causes and reasons for the incident. After careful investigation, possibilities to reduce the risk of a similar incident occurring are explored. A cost-benefit assessment may be carried out to select the most appropriate measures to reduce risk. Examples of measures to reduce risk include:

- establishing new policies
- modifying operating and maintenance procedures
- providing training
- upgrading monitoring and control equipment
- redesigning equipment
- changing material specifications

Business Issues

Other issues such as health, safety, loss control, and customer relations are also addressed in operating and maintenance practices and procedures.

Documentation and reporting—Environmental issues and business activities are often closely related. Environmental issues and concerns are often addressed in an organization's operating and maintenance policies, practices, and procedures manuals.

Governments require that spills and pollution release rates greater than a specific quantity be documented and reported. Environmental test results must also be submitted to government.

Keeping documentation current can be a big task. More importantly, employees must be informed of changes and, in some cases, upgrade training may have to be provided.

Reclamation—Government regulations require that organizations carry out cleanup and reclamation activities as part of normal business and in response to incidents that contaminate the environment (e.g., spills). When business activities that involve extraction of natural resources (e.g., minerals, trees) cease in an area, organizations are required to carry out restoration activities. When facilities such as gas plants, well sites, pipelines, and roads are permanently decommissioned, the area must be restored to its equivalent capability that existed before being disturbed. Some governments require organizations to make a security deposit for reclamation activities. The purpose of the deposit is to ensure that, if a company has financial difficulties in the future, funds are available to carry out the reclamation activities.

Internal audits and continuous improvement—
Organizations may conduct internal audits of their environmental protection system and of the impacts

that their business activities have on the environment. Measurement benchmarks are established so that any changes from the previous audit can be determined. Improvements are noted and deficiencies identified. Corrective action is then determined and implemented.

As part of the commitment to continuous improvement, management reviews of the environmental management program are carried out. Ways and means to further protect the environment are explored and acted upon when feasible. Regular management reviews and internal communication can also increase employee awareness of the organization's commitment to protect the natural environment.

3.3 Elements of an Environmental Management System

A systems approach is often needed to effectively manage the complex environmental aspects of a business and achieve environmental goals. An environmental management systems approach has many elements including:

- stated environmental objectives and policies
- documented system and organizational structure for dealing with environmental issues
- clearly defined employee roles and responsibilities
- methods to monitor and control business activities that potentially impact the environment
- methods to respond to abnormal operating conditions and emergencies
- documented practices and procedures
- record and document control
- training
- measurement benchmarks to determine the effectiveness of environmental protection activities
- internal and external audits
- means to initiate corrective action
- reviews to assess the effectiveness of the environment management system and to determine ways and means to make improvements

Many of the elements listed previously either have an effect on or directly relate to operator and maintenance activities. However, all employees in an organization have a responsibility to understand and respond to environmental issues that relate to their jobs and to support the organization's initiatives to protect the environment.

Check your knowledge

1. Limits established by governments for pollutant release rates are based on _____.
   a. emission rates
   b. time-weighted allowable concentrations
   c. total allowable quantities that can be discharged
   d. all of the above
   e. a and c only

2. Regulations may require the use of monitoring equipment to identify the quantity and type of material being released to the air, water, and land.
   a. true
   b. false

3. The purpose of an environmental impact study is to determine the impact that organizational activities have had or may have in the future on the natural environment.
   a. true
   b. false

4. Industrial companies carrying out activities that might affect groundwater may be required to drill test wells and take samples of the groundwater.
   a. true
   b. false

(continued)

Check your knowledge

5. During processing upsets, emissions and effluents containing excess pollutants may be _____.

   a. reprocessed

   b. diverted to storage tanks

   c. burnt

   d. all of the above

   e. a and b only

6. If an incident occurs that harms the environment, cost is not a factor when selecting measures to reduce the risk of similar incidents.

   a. true

   b. false

7. Environmental test results must be reported to the appropriate government agency.

   a. true

   b. false

8. Government legislation requires that organizations carry out cleanup, remediation, and reclamation activities in response to uncontrolled incidents that contaminate the environment.

   a. true

   b. false

Answers

1. d   2. a   3. a   4. a   5. d   6. b   7. a   8. a

Try this:

1. What environmental protection activities does your organization carry out that you are aware of?

   _____

   _____

   _____

Section 4

Reasons for Protecting the Natural Environment

Organizations comply with the applicable environmental standards for four reasons:

- social responsibility
- regulatory compliance
- due diligence
- public perception (reputation)

4.1 Social Responsibility

Some organizations want to protect the natural environment as well as the safety of workers and the public because they believe it's the right thing to do, not because they have been legislated to do so. Because of their commitment to protecting the environment and people, these organizations may also realize a number of secondary benefits such as lowered operating costs; improved business-to-business, customer, and public relations; improved competitive edge; and expanded market share.

4.2 Regulatory Compliance

Government agencies specify environmental requirements in licenses, permits, letters, or through verbal communication. Failure to comply with environmental requirements may result in fines or legal action against the organization or its officers. To ensure that proper procedures are followed, all personnel within the organization must clearly understand their environmental responsibilities.

Typical examples of activities that organizations carry out to comply with legislated requirements include:
- monitoring stack emissions to the atmosphere
- monitoring effluent discharges to surface waters
- monitoring contaminant levels in soils and groundwater
- incorporating pollution control equipment into process operations
- reclaiming soils contaminated by chemical or petroleum products

4.3 Due Diligence

Due diligence means taking all the necessary steps to demonstrate that environmental policies and procedures are undertaken as an integral part of organizational activities. All employees are responsible for practicing due diligence. Due diligence may be used as a legal defense if it is alleged that negligence within the organization has contributed to environmental damage. An organization may be required to show due diligence to obtain reasonable insurance premiums or financing rates.

Examples of activities demonstrating due diligence include:
- providing written environmental practices and procedures
- documenting environmental training programs, including the demonstration of job skills, and retaining employee training records. The records provide evidence that employees have been properly trained to identify environmental responsibilities and to carry out appropriate environmental procedures.

- documenting maintenance procedures undertaken to limit the possibility of spills from facilities
- providing secondary containment beyond that which is required
- conducting environmental assessments to identify potential liabilities relating to equipment or property bought or sold by the organization
- auditing facilities to ensure proper environmental practices and procedures are followed
- participating in associations and committees dealing with relevant environmental issues

4.4 Public Perception

Organizations wish to be seen as good corporate citizens, concerned about the natural environment and the communities in which they are located. Personnel must be aware of the importance of satisfying public concerns and implementing proper environmental practices for issues affecting the public. Public and employee perception of an organization's attitude towards the environment can be positive or negative. Positive perceptions may enhance the organization's credibility in the community. Negative public sentiment, expressed at public hearings on proposed projects, could cause the government to deny approval for the construction of new facilities. A negative image of the organization's attitude towards the environment may also result in lowered stock values and other organizations being pressured not to do business with that organization.

An organization can be stressed if it perceives itself as doing a good job in protecting the environment but the public or its employees think otherwise. A lack of communication within the organization and with the community or differences in understanding of the community values (e.g., protection of treed areas, use of land resources) can contribute to differences in perception. Organizations can carry out a variety of activities to enhance public perception, including:

- holding public awareness meetings
- conducting tours of company facilities

- publishing information documents and annual environmental management reports outlining the organization's activities
- establishing telephone or e-mail communications so that the public can ask questions and register complaints
- keeping employees informed about the organization's environmental protection activities and initiatives

Check your knowledge

1. Why would a company be concerned about the public's perception of that company's attitude relating to the environment?

   a. the public can influence the government to deny the company approval of new facilities

   b. a negative environmental image could have a negative effect on the value of the company's stock

   c. a negative image could discourage some organizations from doing business with the company

   d. all of the above

   e. a and c only

2. Organizations comply with environmental standards _____.

   a. to prevent being fined

   b. so that due diligence can be used as a legal defense

   c. to develop a positive public perception

   d. because it is the right thing to do and at the same time improve business performance

   e. all of the above

   f. a and b only

   g. c and d only

(continued)

Check your knowledge

3. Providing written environmental procedures, providing environmental training, and keeping training records are all examples of activities demonstrating due diligence.

    a. true
    b. false

Answer

1. d   2. e   3. a

Try this:

1. Organizations have an environmental management program because it is a legislated requirement and/or it makes *good* business sense to do so. Does your organization have an environmental management plan? Why or why not?

    _____

    _____

    _____

    _____

EnviroThink™

34

Job Strategies to Protect the Natural Environment

Environmental protection goals, policies, and practices are usually established at the corporate level. Of concern to management is that employees at the operational levels apply and support corporate environmental protection strategies. Unfortunately, operational staff may find it difficult to effectively support corporate goals, especially in large organizations:

- At the job level, employees may not be aware of the environmental issues that had to be addressed when the organization planned and implemented the environmental protection system. Consequently, employees may not understand the reasons for specific policies, practices, and procedures. By knowing the reasons, employees can appreciate the importance of carrying out work in a specific way and understand the consequences for the environment if the practices and procedures are not followed.
- In organizations where employees have cross-functional roles and responsibilities (working outside of their prime area of expertise), employees may not be aware of the environmental policies, practices, and procedures that apply to their work.

- Employees may be aware of the organization's environmental goals but may have difficulty determining practical ways to apply the goals to their jobs.
- Employees may not recognize that, for some tasks, specific standards and procedural steps have implications for the environment.

All employees in an organization have a responsibility to protect the natural environment. However, the gap between corporate environmental goals and practical job applications could be a problem preventing employees from effectively fulfilling their responsibilities. Several initiatives can help fill the gap:

- making employees aware of the organization's environmental management system
- documenting policies, practices, procedures, and standards for specific jobs and tasks
- providing effective training and supervisory/team leadership to ensure that job activities have a minimal impact on the environment

All these strategies can be effective in contributing to protecting the environment provided there are minimal changes to an employee's roles and responsibilities, work processes and procedures, and work conditions.

Try this:

1. An organization's environmental practices may be written or unwritten. In your job, what are the environmental concerns and what are you expected to do to protect the environment?

   _____

   _____

2. What else could be done in your job to further protect the environment?

   _____

   _____

The Critical Thinking Strategy to Protect the Environment

Because operations staff are often the first ones to identify and carry out the first response to environmental issues, their ability and commitment to protect the environment is important to achieving the organization's environmental goals. Organizations expect their employees to perform at an exemplary level, to be flexible at taking on varied job assignments, and to *think through their work*. To meet those expectations, employees need to use a critical thinking strategy to identify and respond to environmental issues for any job position that they might hold. This section focuses on a critical thinking strategy that involves asking specific questions relating to specific environmental issues.

The critical thinking strategy addresses eleven environmental issues that often apply to operations and maintenance:

Environmental Issues
1   Impact on the natural environment
2.   Pollutant release rates
3.   Measuring and monitoring pollutant releases
4.   Controlling the impact on the environment
5.   Safe disposal of wastes
6.   Protecting the environment when there are technical problems
7.   Minimizing environmental impact when there are emergencies
8.   Keeping informed about organizational activities affecting the environment
9.   Restoring the environment to its intended use
10. Conserving energy
11. Minimizing material consumption

This critical thinking strategy applies to both technical and work processes. Technical processes usually involve starting, monitoring, adjusting, and shutting down production systems. Work processes usually involve using tools and equipment to carry out a task or do a job. For work processes, the critical thinking strategy to protect the environment can be used before, during, and after completing the work.

Each environmental issue is presented as a question. Because technical and work processes are somewhat different, the question associated with each issue has been worded in two ways. If the wording of a question does not fit well with your particular job circumstances, reword the question. You can also reword the questions to make them more personalized. Examples of wording the questions in a way that focuses on you and your responsibilities are given in the following sections that address each question.

Critical Thinking Strategy to Protect the Environment		
Environmental Issue	**Technical Process Question**	**Work Process Question**
1. **Impact on the natural environment**	Does the process have the potential to affect the environment?	Is there anything that can cause harm to the environment?
2. **Pollutant release rates**	What are the allowable pollutant release rates and quantities?	How much material can be released, disposed of, or harvested without harming the environment?
3. **Measuring and monitoring pollutant releases**	How are pollutant releases measured or monitored?	What are the types and specifications of the equipment used to measure and monitor pollutant releases?
4. **Controlling the impact on the environment**	What technical controls are being used to limit environmental impact?	What are the types and specifications of the equipment used to limit the impact on the environment?
5. **Safe disposal of wastes**	What methods are used to dispose of wastes generated by the processes?	How are hazardous and non-hazardous wastes stored and disposed of?
6. **Protecting the environment when there are technical problems**	What has to be done to limit the impact that process upsets or equipment failure could have on the environment?	What contingencies can be put in place to deal with unexpected problems or equipment failure that could impact the environment?
7. **Minimizing environmental impact when there are emergencies**	How does your organization respond to emergencies?	When doing work, what contingencies can be put in place to deal with emergency situations?
8. **Keeping informed about organizational activities affecting the environment**	What environmental reports are required by external agencies?	When doing work, what documentation is required if an incident has a negative impact on the environment?

(continued)

Critical Thinking Strategy to Protect the Environment		
Environmental Issue	Technical Process Question	Work Process Question
9. **Restoring the environment to its intended use**	What environmental cleanup or reclamation activities are required?	What can be done to clean up a spill or leak?
10. **Conserving energy**	What technical and operational changes can be made to reduce energy use?	What changes can be made to work processes to reduce energy consumption?
11. **Minimizing material consumption**	What technical adjustments can be made to reduce material consumption?	What changes can be made to the work processes to minimize material use?

You ask yourself the eleven questions to determine if there are any related environmental issues. In some cases, a *no* answer to the first question eliminates the need to ask several other questions.

If there is an environmental issue, you need to find the answer to the question. You can use a variety of sources to get answers that will determine the best way to protect the environment:
- operator and maintenance reference manuals
- operator and maintenance practices and procedures
- waste storage and disposal guidelines
- environmental, health, and safety manuals
- Material Safety Data Sheets (MSDS)
- other employees
- environmental specialists

ISSUE 1   Impact on the natural environment

Process Question

Technical	Does the process have the potential to affect the environment?
Work	Is there anything that can cause harm to the environment?

Any action that removes, modifies, or adds to the air, water, or land can have an impact on the natural environment.

What occurs in one component (air, water, or land) may also affect another component. For example, toxic rain from the atmosphere may contaminate land as well as surface waters in lakes and rivers.

Air Quality

Pollutants can modify chemical or physical components present in the air or can be carried by the air to impact water and land. Air pollution may cause human health concerns and damage to wildlife, vegetation, and other living organisms.

Impacts to air quality may occur in the upper atmosphere or near the earth's surface as well as on a local or global scale.

In the upper atmosphere, the release of compounds such as chlorofluorocarbons contributes to depleting the ozone layer. Increased levels of methane and carbon dioxide in the atmosphere are thought to contribute to global warming. The term *carbon footprint* refers to the discharge of carbon-dioxide and other carbon-based gases into the environment.

Air Emissions: *material released to the air that may have minimal environmental impact because of its physical, chemical, or biological nature, or may be treated to minimize environmental impact*

Near the earth's surface, smog produced from vehicle emissions, industrial activities, and the heating of buildings can affect human health. Burning wastes such as sawdust at lumber mills produces ash, increasing the particulate in the atmosphere. Volcanic eruptions can discharge large amounts of ash into the atmosphere. The ash can drift great distances to affect a large area.

At the local level, airborne chemicals can affect respiration and cause allergic reactions. High noise levels or odors can disturb the public and wildlife.

Water Quality

Water quality can be affected by changes to the *chemical, physical,* or *biological* properties of water located on or below the earth's surface. Water pollution may also affect human health and damage aquatic organisms and vegetation. Damage to aquatic resources and extinction of aquatic species may result from over-harvesting and other human activities. Examples of changes to the chemical, physical, and biological properties of water are provided on the following page.

41

Chemical

- Effluent releases that introduce particulate matter into a river or raise the water temperature.
- Accidental spills that introduce harmful chemicals into the waterbody.
- Pesticides, herbicides, and fertilizers inappropriately applied to agricultural land and septic releases to fields can seep deep into the ground, contaminating groundwater.
- Accidental spills of chemicals or petroleum products as well as liquids released from normal industrial processes can contaminate both surface and groundwater.
- Chemicals can coat birds causing the birds to freeze, die of heat stress, ingest poisonous compounds in an attempt to clean their feathers, or lose their ability to fly.

Physical

- Changes to the quantity of water can also affect the quality of the water. Overuse of groundwater and reduced surface water levels can severely affect the quality of the groundwater. Reductions in water flow in rivers due to seasonal and climate changes or human intervention (e.g., irrigation) can affect the ability of the rivers to cope with effluent discharges.

- Dams on rivers permanently change the ecology of the river. Controlled releases of water during spring or rainy seasons reduce flooding.

- A reduction in seasonal flooding of rivers can adversely affect the ecology of river deltas.
- Reduction in water levels in swamps, sloughs, and lakes affects aquatic and land species.

Biological

- Sewage releases or water runoff that introduce harmful micro-organisms into a waterbody.
- Changes to the temperature of the water can affect the ecology. For example, the addition of warm water to a lake can promote algae growth. Decomposition of algae can lead to a reduction of oxygen in the water, affecting other species.
- Diseases can accidentally be transmitted to the natural environment. For example, fish hatcheries can become contaminated with infectious diseases. If diseased fish stock escape a hatchery, the disease can spread to other fish.

Because accidental spills have the potential of causing significant environmental damage and harm to human health, extensive assessment, cleanup, and site restoration activities may be required.

Land Quality

In addition to changing air and water quality, changes to the chemical, physical, or biological properties (e.g., plants and animal) of the land surface or subsurface can affect the environment.

Chemical

- Human health can be affected when harmful chemicals absorbed by plants and animals are passed up the food chain.
- Introduction of non-degradable herbicides into soil may sterilize soils, limiting vegetation growth and causing possible wind erosion.
- Accidental spills of chemicals or petroleum products can have major impacts on land quality, with the potential for extensive damage to soil quality, land resources, and groundwater. Site assessment, remediation, and reclamation procedures may be required to return the land to acceptable environmental conditions.

Physical

Direct impacts to land may occur in various ways:

- Indiscriminate mining of mineral resources can damage sensitive areas, resulting in the extinction of endangered species.
- Physical changes to the contour of the land surface can change water drainage patterns, causing water erosion, flooding, drainage of wetlands, and contamination of surface and groundwater.
- Roads, cutlines, and changes in land use can affect wildlife migration patterns.
- Non-sustainable use of land resources can severely affect the ecosystem. Indiscriminate clear cutting of timber destroys wildlife habitat and can cause soil erosion. The washing of eroded soil into streams affects aquatic life. Without trees to control water shed, flooding can become a problem. In recent years, concerns have been expressed that extensive removal of vegetation from the earth's surface can limit the earth's ability to absorb carbon dioxide from the atmosphere. Increased quantities of carbon dioxide in the atmosphere are thought to contribute to global warming.

Biological

- Land pollution can contaminate soil and groundwater resources, and can affect wildlife, vegetation, and other living organisms in the surrounding area.

- Changes to soil structure or texture from mixing topsoil with subsoil may reduce soil productivity in agricultural areas.

Impacts to land resources may be managed responsibly through sustainable development and the controlled use of natural resources. Sustainable development allows a resource to be renewed and developed on a continuous basis. Fish, trees, and mushrooms are examples of natural resources which may undergo sustainable development if they are properly managed.

Any activity that removes, modifies, or adds to air, water, or land can have an impact on the natural environment as shown in the following table.

Action	Environmental Component		
	Air	Water	Land
Remove	effect on quality	effect on quality	effect on quality
Modify	effect on quality	effect on quality	effect on quality
Add	effect on quality	effect on quality	effect on quality

Before, during, and after completing work, determine if there are any possible environmental impacts. You can ask yourself the technical or work process questions stated at the beginning of this section:
- Does the process have the potential to affect the environment?
- Is there anything that can cause harm to the environment?

You can reword the question to fit better for you and your workplace. For example:
- Do the work situation and my actions remove, modify, or add to air, water, or land?

• Are there any activities that remove, modify, or add to air, water, or land?

If the answer is *yes*, then determine if acceptable limits are exceeded (Issue 2).

The following examples are provided to help you identify some of the possible environmental impacts that can be created in workplaces.

Remove — Air

There are very few work situations in which components of air could be removed in large enough quantities to affect the natural environment. However, in confined spaces and mines, the removal of oxygen can be a serious safety hazard.

Remove — Water

• Drainage of wetland, swamp, and muskeg areas can severely modify the ecosystem, harming wildlife and waterfowl habitats in the surrounding area.
• High consumption of water for industrial, home, and agricultural use can deplete rivers and lakes, modifying the ecosystem and harming aquatic life.
• Over-fishing can endanger aquatic species in oceans, rivers, and lakes.

Ecosystem:

a community of living things and its physical and chemical environment

Remove — Land

• Over-hunting can endanger wildlife.
• Open pit mining removes the overburden to expose the ore which is then removed. Removal of overburden can damage the surrounding ecosystem by changing the surrounding site contours. Changing contours can change drainage patterns, modify groundwater flow patterns, and erode the surrounding areas.

- Intensive agricultural growing practices can decrease soil productivity, contributing to land erosion. Dust storms can cause millions of tonnes (tons) of topsoil to be displaced each year.

Modify — Air
- Surface level ozone may be formed by the reaction of components in smog, affecting public health.
- Airborne chemicals, directly or by reacting with other chemicals, can affect respiration, cause allergic reactions, and potentially cause cancer.

Modify — Water
- Cooling water discharged into lakes and rivers can increase the local water temperature. Algae blooms may increase, depleting oxygen in the water and affecting fish and vegetation.

- Surface water run-off containing agricultural fertilizers can increase nutrient levels in the water, causing algae blooms and reducing the level of oxygen in the water.
- Settling ponds from industrial operations may attract birds which become poisoned by ingesting toxins in the ponds. Birds may also be covered with material which coats their feathers.

Modify — Land

- Topsoil properties and texture may be modified by mixing topsoil with subsoil during pipeline construction, decreasing the productivity of the soil.
- Tailings from ore processing mills change the terrain and soil composition in the surrounding area.
- An oil spill onto land can change the texture, water absorbing capabilities, and chemical properties of the soil, changing the population of micro-organisms in the soil and limiting growth of vegetation in the affected area.
- Recontouring during construction can result in soil erosion, draining of wetland areas, and water pooling or flooding in unintended areas.
- Changes in land use can change the ecology of an area. For example, changing native grassland to agricultural use can endanger native grassland species; clearing forests for farming can affect wildlife habitat. Cities often grow outwards, changing the ecology of the area.
- Power lines, cut lines, rights-of-way, and roads affect animal foraging and migration patterns.

Add — Air

Air Emissions:

material released to the air that may have minimal environmental impact because of its physical, chemical, or biological nature, or may be treated to minimize environmental impact

- Burning coal in coal-fired steam power plants can cause sulfur dioxide emissions to be added to the atmosphere. Sulfur dioxide can combine with moisture in the air to form acids, changing the acidity of lakes and soils.
- Oil and gas production from battery and refining operations can release hydrogen sulfide to the atmosphere, creating noxious odors and contributing to acid rain production.
- Gasoline and diesel internal combustion engines release carbon monoxide, carbon dioxide, and nitrogen dioxide to the atmosphere, creating smog. Poorly operating internal combustion engines can add additional carbon monoxide, carbon dioxide, and oxides of nitrogen to the atmosphere.
- Unplanned vapor leaks (fugitive emissions) from piping and equipment such as valves and pumps impact the environment. Other sources of emissions include vents from tanks and sumps, fume hoods, and fans, spray cans, and collection ponds.
- Emissions from these sources impact the environment by:
  - adding vapors to the air which may precipitate to the land and water
  - creating noise which disturbs neighbors, livestock, and wildlife
  - causing unpleasant odors
- Metal particulate from smelting and ore processing operations can be released to the atmosphere and contaminate soils and water in the surrounding area.
- High noise levels from industrial operations could result in noise complaints from the public and disturb wildlife.
- Lights and noise, from roads, cities, and industrial facilities, disturb animals.

Add — Water

- Raw and processed sewage from homes is disposed of in lakes, rivers, and oceans. The sewage can reduce the oxygen content in the water and provide nutrients which promote algae and plant growth.
- Pulp and paper mills discharge chlorine into lakes and rivers. Reactive forms of chlorine are toxic to aquatic life

and can form stable chlorinated organic compounds in the environment that are a concern to human and animal health.

- Various manufacturing processes discharge processed water containing solid particulate into lakes and rivers, increasing turbidity in the water.
- Salts applied to city streets can dissolve in surface water run-off and increase salinity in freshwater lakes, rivers, and soil.
- Mercury from mine tailings and other operations can migrate into lakes and streams and be converted into methyl mercury, which can accumulate in fish and vegetation. Methyl mercury poses a chronic health hazard to humans if they eat contaminated fish or vegetation.
- Petroleum products released from spills or leaks can float on groundwater and contaminate water supplies. Benzene, toluene, ethyl benzene, and xylene (BTEX) can dissolve in water, posing a wildlife and public health hazard.
- Chemicals discharged as by-products of industrial operations can be toxic to aquatic life and can contaminate groundwater, posing a public health hazard.

Add — Land

- Fertilizers, herbicides, and pesticides can seep through the soil, contaminate groundwater, and can migrate with surface water run-off into rivers and lakes. Herbicides applied to soil for long-term vegetation control can migrate with water run-off into agricultural fields, sterilizing productive soils and limiting growth of agricultural crops.

- Chemicals and metals from materials disposed of in landfill sites can leach into the soil and contaminate groundwater. Garbage disposed of in landfills can present aesthetic concerns (e.g., odors and unsightly conditions) and can produce methane gas which can contribute to global warming.
- Chemicals from slow-leaking pipes and control valves can accumulate in the soil over several years, requiring extensive and costly cleanup.

Whenever a process or activity removes, modifies, or adds to air, water, or land, determine if there is potential for damaging the environment. Government regulations, permits, and licenses specify the standards for your organization's activities. This information should be available if it relates to your job.

Continuous and sporadic waste-generating processes

Waste-generating processes which affect the environment can be classified into two categories:

- *continuous* processes which result from ongoing organizational activities that release pollutants to the environment
- *sporadic* processes which usually result from disposal of waste products which can no longer be used within the organization

Pollutant:

material that interferes with the natural functioning of an ecosystem

The following table provides examples of waste generation processes that affect the environment.

Processes with Continuous Impact	Processes with Sporadic Impact
• Flare and furnace stacks release gases and solid particles into the atmosphere. • Effluent pipes discharge liquid and suspended solids into the water. • Discharge pipes from mining processes dump liquid tailings into ponds. • Pumps transfer process water to deep wells.	**Disposal of:** • process filters • spent catalysts • used oil, glycols, and wiping rags • soaps and detergents • solvents and paints • seals on floating roof oil storage tanks

(continued)

Processes with Continuous Impact	Processes with Sporadic Impact
• Large mobile equipment harvests trees and clears land. • Nets, traps, and harvesting equipment remove marine life from rivers, lakes, and oceans. • Powered spreaders distribute manure over the land. • Sewage systems and containers transfer by-products from food processing and preparation to water and land disposal sites.	**Disposal of:** • demolished facilities and construction waste • PCB-contaminated transformer oils • radioactive materials • biomedical wastes • herbicides or pesticides which can no longer be used • chemical- or pesticide-contaminated containers **Note:** Incidents and emergency conditions such as equipment leaks, spills, and fires can also have an impact on the environment

Depending on the particular industry and job, a process classified as sporadic could be classified as continuous or vice versa. Of special concern are those processes that are sporadic, for example, operating and maintenance tasks that are performed occasionally. Because the work may occur infrequently, you may not recognize that there is an impact on the environment or know the specific disposal practices that must be followed. Some organizations have housekeeping policies and procedures and waste storage and disposal guidelines that identify situations that could have an impact on the environment.

While *doing* the work, you can:
• consider the consequences for the natural environment of a condition, action, or event
• determine the environmental reasons why particular steps of a procedure are required

If an activity has the potential of affecting the environment, you need to know the acceptable limits for removing or adding products to the environment (Issue 2).

<table>
<tr><td>LEARNING
ACTIVITY</td><td>1</td></tr>
</table>

Impact on the natural environment

Does the process have the potential to harm the environment?

Is there anything that can cause harm to the environment?

1a.   Rewrite the question for Issue 1 to suit you, your job, and your workplace. For example, *Are there any activities that remove, modify, or add to air, water, or land?* Write your question in the table in the Job Aid at the end of this book.

1b.   On each of the following tables:
   - list an activity of your organization that removes, modifies, or adds to air, water, or land
   - check the box(es) to indicate how the activity affects the environment (removes, modifies, or adds to the environment)
   - check the box(es) to indicate the environmental component(s) that are affected
   - classify each *activity* as continuous or sporadic
   - identify the impact that each situation could have on the natural environment

Organizational activity	Action on environment	Environmental component	Continuous or sporadic	Specific impact on environment
	☐ remove ☐ modify ☐ add	☐ air ☐ water ☐ land	☐ continuous ☐ sporadic	

Organizational activity	Action on environment	Environmental component	Continuous or sporadic	Specific impact on environment
	☐ remove ☐ modify ☐ add	☐ air ☐ water ☐ land	☐ continuous ☐ sporadic	

1c. On the table below, state a task or job that you do which impacts on the environment. Complete the table.

Your task or job	Action on environment	Environmental component	Continuous or sporadic	Specific impact on environment
	☐ remove ☐ modify ☐ add	☐ air ☐ water ☐ land	☐ continuous ☐ sporadic	

ISSUE 2 — Pollutant release rates

Process Question

Technical	What are the allowable pollutant release rates and quantities?
Work	How much material can be released, disposed of, or harvested without harming the environment?

Many types of human activity impact the environment. The goal is to control human activities in ways that sustain the environment. The most obvious type of human activity that can harm the environment is adding pollutants and wastes to air, water, and land. Pollution is the contamination of the environment with substances or energy that interfere with human health, the quality of life, or the natural functioning of an ecosystem. Wastes are materials that cannot be treated within the organization in an effective manner or can no longer be used for their original purpose and require disposal. Wastes are classified as being hazardous or non-hazardous and can be in the form of a gas, liquid, dust, or solid. Some pollutants and wastes are treated before disposal to make them less harmful to the environment.

Many methods are used to dispose of pollutants and wastes:
- discharge into the atmosphere (air emissions)
- discharge into water (effluent)
- transport to a landfill

- exchange with another organization that can make use of the materials (recycling)
- Governments have established standards to limit the quantities and rates at which specific products can be added to air, water, and land to minimize harm to the environment.

Sustainable Development:

carry out business activities in a way that maintains the ecology

Limits for pollutants are based on scientific research undertaken to measure environmental toxicity. Limits for sustainable development are also based on studies undertaken to determine sustainable development rates. Toxicological tests of a compound to determine its long-term chronic effects and potential for causing cancer are difficult to perform. Interpreting the test results with certainty can also be difficult. Because it can be very costly to carry out a complete toxicological test of a compound, rigorous toxicological tests are not applied to all compounds.

Limits established by the government for pollutant release may be based on:
- total allowable quantity that can be discharged
- time-weighted allowable concentrations
- emission/discharge rates

Variations in allowable release limits may also be based on seasonal conditions. For example, releases of effluent to a river may be reduced in winter because a river's flow rate in winter is slower than in summer.

Regulatory limits or standards are incorporated into operating licenses or environmental permits. Typical examples of regulatory limits related to pollutant release include the following:

- limits on airborne compounds set as a maximum quantity per hour or per day. Airborne compounds include sulfur dioxide, hydrogen sulfide, oxides of nitrogen, carbon monoxide, total particulate, or heavy metals.
- limits on chemical compounds allowed to be discharged into a river based on a maximum quantity per hour or per day
- limits on chemical compounds allowed to be discharged into a river based on an assessment of the general water quality or water potability. Assessment of quality or potability may include turbidity, biochemical oxygen demand, chemical oxygen demand, total nitrogen, total sulfates, and total heavy metals.

Governments allow organizations to exceed the normal allowable emission rates or discharge limits during specific operating conditions. For example, during startups and shutdowns of processes, the quantity of emissions or effluents may increase because of the inefficiency of the process during that period.

Rates for Sustainable Development

Limits on sustainable development are imposed to minimize damage to the ecosystem. Limits established for sustainable development may be based on total quantity of resources which may be removed from the ecosystem within a specified time period or from a specified area. Limits are set based on the environment's ability to recover. For example, fish reproduce, thereby replenishing the fish stock but, if there is over-fishing, stock can be depleted.

Regulatory limits for resource use may be incorporated into environmental permits or licenses to minimize damage to the ecosystem.

Typical examples of regulatory limits related to resource management include:

- limits on the type and amount of timber which can be logged from an area

(continued)

Rates for Sustainable Development
• limits on the type and quantity of fish which can be harvested from freshwater or marine environment. Limits may also specify the period when fishing is permitted. • limits on the amount of water that can be removed from lakes and rivers. Removal rates may also vary according to the season.

LEARNING ACTIVITY 2

Pollutant release rates

What are the allowable pollutant release rates and quantities?

How much material can be released, disposed of, or harvested without harming the environment?

2a.   Rewrite the question for Issue 2 to suit you, your job, and your workplace. For example, *How much of a change (amount of release, removal) can be done without harming the environment?* Write your question in the table in the Job Aid at the end of this book.

Your organization's activities may or may not involve releases of pollutants into the air, water, or land. If your organization does not release pollutants, work/consult with someone who works for an organization that releases pollutants.

2b.   Identify a release of a pollutant to the environment.

_____

_____

2c.   The limit for the pollutant release is based on:

☐ total allowable quantity that can be discharged

☐ time-weighted allowable concentrations

☐ emission rates

2d. Where would you find information identifying the regulated allowable limit?

_____

2e. Not all pollutants released to the atmosphere are regulated and measured. For example, idling vehicles release pollutants but the amount of releases are usually not monitored and measured. To what extent do you agree or disagree with the following statement. Explain your position. There should be strong regulations and enforcement regarding the amount of time a vehicle idles.

_____

_____

_____

2f. Identify the type of sustainable natural resource that is being removed from the environment in your province or state.

_____

2g. Where would you find information on the quantity/rate of the sustainable natural resource the government allows to be removed from the environment?

_____

ISSUE 3	Measuring and monitoring pollutant releases

Process Question

Technical	How are pollutant releases measured or monitored?
Work	What are the types and specifications of the equipment used to measure and monitor pollutant releases?

Regulations may require the organization to use monitoring equipment to identify the quantity and type of material being released to the air, water, and land. Discharge rates of air emissions and effluents can be continuously monitored or sampled on a regular basis. Regulated limits are not to be exceeded. The test results must be documented and reported to a government agency.

Depending on the situation, a variety of methods can be used to monitor discharge or emission rates, including:
- using continuous air monitoring equipment mounted on stacks or in dedicated air monitoring stations located downwind of a facility. Air monitoring equipment can identify the quantity and types of materials being released to the atmosphere. Information is recorded on-site and may be electronically transmitted to off-site personnel. Visual or audible alarms or telephone notification alarms are normally incorporated into air monitors. These alarm systems ensure that proper personnel are notified as quickly as possible should monitored parameters exceed specified limits.
- recording the total quantity of effluent being released
- sampling effluent before discharge to water using grab sampling or composite sampling
  - Grab sampling involves taking an individual sample at a designated location and time for laboratory analysis. The resulting sample represents the composition of the effluent at a specific time.
  - Composite sampling involves continually collecting small samples in a container over a specific period. The total sample in the container, which represents the average composition of the effluent stream over a given time period, is analyzed.
  - Grab or composite samples may be taken manually or with automated samplers.

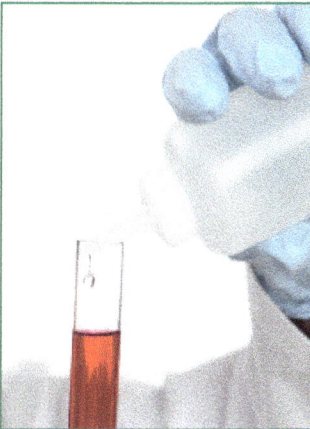

Depending on the circumstances, a variety of measurements determine the degree of contamination and/or environmental impact that organizational activities have on the environment. Noise also impacts the environment. Noise can be monitored by:
- noise metering
- tracking public complaints

After identifying the methods used to monitor releases, you may need to know how to determine when releases approach or exceed regulated limits. You may also have to be able to prevent exceeding limits and to respond effectively when limits are exceeded (Issue 7).

Monitoring removal of sustainable natural resources

Various methods are used to monitor and control the removal of sustainable natural resources such as timber, fish, and water:

- licensing and identification
- quotas and permits
- harvest inspections
- product tagging
- transportation load inspections
- product quantity measurements
- storage inspections
- point of sale inspections

LEARNING ACTIVITY 3

Measuring and monitoring pollutant releases

How are pollutant releases measured or monitored?

What are the types and specifications of the equipment used to measure and monitor pollutant releases?

3a. Rewrite the question for Issue 3 to suit you, your job, and your workplace. For example, *How do I know how much is being released (how extensive are the changes)?* Write your question in the table in the Job Aid at the end of this book.

Your organization's activities may or may not involve releases of pollutants into the air, water, or land. If your organization does not release pollutants, work/consult with someone who works for an organization that releases pollutants.

3b. Identify the methods used at your site to monitor releases to the environment.

_____

_____

_____

3c. For each release, identify the method(s) used to determine that regulatory release limits are being approached or exceeded._____

_____

_____

3d. If a release approaches the regulatory limit, what action do you take to prevent the limit from being exceeded?

_____

_____

_____

3e. Identify the measurements your organization takes to determine the amount of contaminants in the natural environment.

_____

_____

_____

3f. Identify the types of impact studies or surveys your organization undertakes to determine the impact that organizational activities have on the natural environment.

_____

_____

_____

3g. Identify the method(s) used to measure the quantity of sustainable natural resources being removed from the natural environment.

_____

_____

3h. What are the methods used to determine when the regulatory limits for removal of sustainable natural resources are being approached?

_____

_____

_____

ISSUE 4	Controlling the impact on the environment

Process Question

Technical	What technical controls are being used to limit environmental impact?
Work	What are the types and specifications of the equipment used to limit the impact on the environment?

Both pollutant and waste-minimizing practices can reduce the harmful affects on the natural environment.

Three methods for minimizing the impact of pollutants on the environment include:
- minimizing the generation of pollutants by adjusting production equipment in response to changing operating conditions
- removing pollutants from the discharge stream
- modifying pollutants so that they have a less harmful effect on the environment

The type of technology used to minimize the quantity and toxicity of pollutants depends on the properties and characteristics of the polluting materials:
- gases
- liquids
- dusts
- solids

Gases

Process gases and gases produced by furnaces and internal combustion engines may contain products that are toxic to the environment. For instance, in the oil and gas industry, hydrogen sulfide is a gas commonly found with hydrocarbons.

Sulfur recovery systems convert the hydrogen sulfide to sulfur and sulfur dioxide. After conversion, small quantities of hydrogen sulfide which may still be present are monitored by gas sampling equipment located downstream of the sulfur recovery unit. Based on the measurements, the sulfur recovery system automatically makes adjustments to maximize sulfur recovery and minimize the quantity that will be released to atmosphere. Gases from the sulfur recovery unit then go to an incinerator to be burned and released to atmosphere.

Gases directed to a flare stack may contain entrained liquids (liquid droplets suspended in the gas). Before the gases enter the flare stack, they can be passed through a knockout drum or scrubber to remove the liquids. The liquids can then be reprocessed or disposed of in deep disposal wells.

On internal combustion engines, oxygen sensors detect the quantity of oxygen in the exhaust gases. A computer uses the information from the sensors to adjust the engine's fuel-to-air ratio to minimize pollution.

Liquids

Liquids from industrial processes may be treated before discharge to the environment. Treatment processes for liquid effluent could include:

- filtering to remove suspended particulate
- settling to remove suspended solids

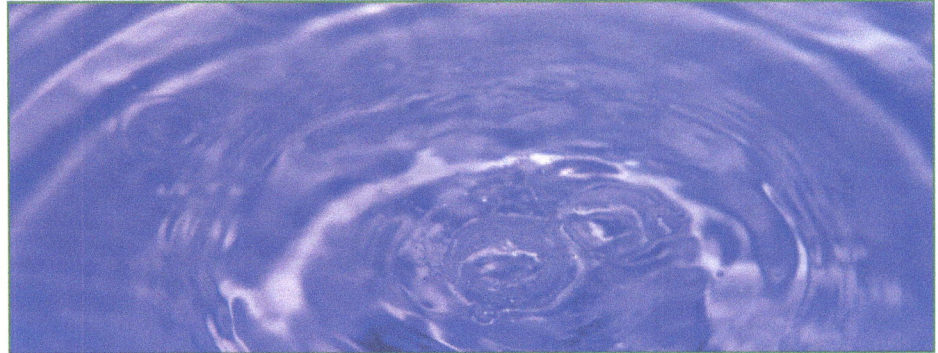

- converting dissolved compounds to compounds that settle by:
  - adsorbing dissolved chemical materials in water using activated carbon or synthetic chemical resins
  - aerating to promote microbial action and break down dissolved chemical compounds
  - adjusting the acidity/alkalinity (pH) of the water to precipitate out metals
  - chemically reacting hazardous materials in the effluent to convert or remove these materials
- breaking down chemical compounds using ultraviolet radiation
- decomposing sewage components using both aerobic and anaerobic bacteria
- disinfecting using oxidants (e.g., chlorine, ozone) and ultraviolet light to kill bacteria or micro-organisms in the effluent
- neutralizing (adjusting the pH) of acidic or alkaline materials in the effluent before release

Produced water is water that is naturally found with the oil and gas produced from oil and gas wells. The produced water is separated from the oil and gas and discharged to a water body or injected back into the formation if quality standards are met. Generally, industry prefers to inject produced water into

the formation from which it was taken. If the produced water is reinjected, the water must be compatible with the formation water to minimize damage to the formation. Before injection, the produced water may have to be treated. Several possible treating methods are:
- filtering to remove solids
- adding chemicals to adjust the pH (acidity/alkalinity)
- adding biocides to kill bacteria

Dust

Solid particles contained in flue gases and exhaust air can be removed by mechanical devices which include:
- cyclones
- bag filters
- electrostatic precipitators

Solids

Solids generated from industrial processes may be remediated and returned to the environment or disposed of in an approved landfill. Quality standards must be met. Different landfills are approved for different types/concentrations of wastes.

Treatment processes for solid materials may include:
- washing with an appropriate solvent to remove surface contamination
- autoclaving or incinerating biohazardous solid materials
- bioremediating contaminated soils using nutrients, oxygen, and water to enhance microbial action and break down petroleum products or chemicals in the soil

Environmental permits dictate the type of products that can be released to the environment and the quantity of the products released over specific time intervals (e.g., 4 hours, 8 hours, 24 hours).

Pollution controls must operate effectively and reliably to meet the requirements of the environmental permits. Equipment failure could result in releases exceeding regulated limits. Prompt response to abnormal equipment operation or failure is required (Issue 6).

LEARNING ACTIVITY 4

Controlling the impact on the environment

What technical controls are being used to limit environmental impact?

What are the types and specifications of the equipment used to limit the impact on the environment?

4a. Rewrite the question for Issue 4 to suit you, your job, and your workplace. For example, *How can I limit the impact on the environment (how can I control the amount of materials being released)?* Write your question in the table in the Job Aid at the end of this book.

Your organization's activities may or may not involve controlling releases of pollutants into the air, land, or water. If your organization does not release pollutants, work/consult with someone who is familiar with pollution control equipment.

4b. Identify the types of pollutants or wastes that your organization releases to the environment.

_____

_____

_____

4c. Identify your organization's methods to minimize the impact of the pollutants on the environment (e.g., incinerate).

_____

_____

_____

4d. Identify pollution control equipment in your job or organization.

_____

_____

_____

4e. Describe the most likely causes for pollutant release rates to exceed the permitted amount (e.g., burner quits in an incinerator).

_____

_____

_____

_____

ISSUE 5	Safe disposal of wastes

Process Question

Technical	What methods are used to dispose of waste generated by the processes?
Work	How are hazardous and non-hazardous wastes stored and disposed?

Wastes are materials that cannot be treated within the organization in an effective manner or can no longer be used for their original purpose and require disposal. Wastes are generally classified as being hazardous or non-hazardous and can be in the form of a gas, liquid, slurry, dust, or solid. Some wastes are treated before disposal to make them safer to handle and/or less harmful to the environment.

NOTE

In this book, the term *hazardous waste* describes any waste with properties that are potentially harmful to living organisms or to the environment. No precise jurisdictional definition is intended.

Many methods are used to dispose of wastes:
- discharge into the atmosphere (air emissions)
- discharge into water (effluent)
- transport to a landfill or treatment facility
- exchange with another organization that can make use of the materials

In this book, the safe disposal of wastes uses the term wastes to mean those wastes that usually require off-site disposal.

The key issues associated with wastes are:
- classification
- handling
- on-site storage
- disposal
- transportation
- documentation

Waste Disposal

Wastes usually require off-site disposal. Wastes generated by an organization must be properly identified and classified as hazardous or non-hazardous. Government legislation specifies waste characterization criteria and analytical procedures for proper waste classification before disposal.

Environmental disposal requirements, especially for hazardous wastes, are heavily regulated by government agencies. Regulations specify the handling, storage, transport, disposal, and documentation requirements for hazardous wastes. The larger the quantity of hazardous wastes stored on-site, the more potential there is for a spill or leak to cause harm to the environment. If there is a spill or leak of a hazardous substance, an immediate and effective response is required to minimize the impact on the environment and protect the health and safety of personnel (Issue 7).

Hazardous Wastes

Hazardous wastes are substances or materials which may affect the health of living organisms or cause damage to the environment if they are released directly to the environment. Hazardous wastes require proper disposal in compliance with federal, provincial/state, and municipal regulations.

Classification—Classification of hazardous wastes can vary from jurisdiction to jurisdiction. Wastes that are typically classified as hazardous include:

- waste gases which are flammable, non-flammable, compressed, corrosive, toxic, or ozone-depleting and can no longer be used for their original purpose
- waste liquids which are flammable
- waste solids which are flammable, spontaneously combustible, or water reactive
- waste materials which produce excessive amounts of oxygen through release or chemical reaction, causing spontaneous combustion of surrounding materials (known as oxidizers)
- waste solids or liquids which are poisonous or toxic
- biomedical wastes which cannot be treated on-site
- waste radioactive materials
- waste corrosive solids or liquids
- waste materials with miscellaneous hazardous properties such as polychlorinated biphenyls (PCBs)
- materials which contain leachable toxic wastes that can contaminate soil or groundwater
- non-hazardous wastes which are contaminated with hazardous wastes

Leachable:

material that is soluble in water and can filter down through the soil

Both production and maintenance activities may involve hazardous wastes. Used oil, oily rags, used amine filters, and cleaning solvents associated with maintenance activities are examples of wastes that may be classified as hazardous.

Taking into account all the different types of industry, the list of hazardous wastes is very extensive.

Handling—Hazardous wastes pose health and safety risks. Specific Personal Protective Equipment (PPE) such as respirators and rubber gloves may be required to handle wastes.

WARNING

Hazardous wastes pose health and safety risks. Refer to the Material Safety Data Sheet (MSDS) for a specific substance to get information about hazards and precautions.

Storage—Government regulations specify that hazardous wastes must be properly stored on-site. The larger the quantity of hazardous wastes stored on-site, the more potential there is for a spill or leak to cause harm to the environment. Specific types of containers may be required to handle and store waste (e.g., wastes that contain acids or solvents). The containers must not deteriorate when exposed to these chemicals. Waste containers are often placed on catch pans to contain any waste should the container leak.

Legislation or permits may limit the amount of waste which may be stored on-site. Storage site design criteria may be listed in the legislation which regulates the organization, or listed in environmental licenses or permits for the organization.

Disposal methods—In most jurisdictions, the facility generating the waste must be registered as a hazardous waste generator with a provincial, state, or county agency. Government regulations specify methods to treat hazardous and non-hazardous wastes to reduce their impact on the environment. Specific methods for disposal may have to be used.

A proper disposal method and/or treatment method must be identified for the waste before disposal. Typical disposal and treatment methods of hazardous wastes include:
- incineration in high temperature incinerators
- chemical treatment to neutralize or convert the waste into chemical compounds which have minimal hazard to the environment

- solidification of hazardous liquid or solid wastes into a material which is not leachable
- thermal desorption to release hazardous materials contained in activated carbon used in process filters
- distilling of contaminated solvents to remove hazardous waste contaminants
- landfilling solid hazardous wastes in secure lined landfills which are monitored for leachate on a continual basis
- re-refining motor oils to remove heavy metals
- long-term safe storage of radioisotopes until they decay to a safe product(s)

Poor waste handling and/or disposal practices can seriously contaminate the soil:

- Never pour wastes such as used solvents and oils on the ground. At some old facilities, it was a common practice to dump used oils, solvents, and cleaners outside the back door or in a corner of a lot.
- Contamination can occur because of organizational activities such as sandblasting of equipment. Over time, the soil can become contaminated with heavy metals.
- Underground tanks may develop slow leaks that are not detected. Over several years, the surrounding soil and water table can become seriously contaminated.

Before an industrial property is sold, an environmental assessment is commonly performed. If the site is contaminated, the owner is responsible for cleaning up the property at his or her own expense.

Transportation and documentation—After a proper disposal method for the waste is identified, hazardous wastes must be transported to the disposal site in compliance with federal Transportation of Dangerous Goods (TDG) regulations or the regulations specific to the jurisdiction. The regulations require the use of a hazardous waste shipping manifest, specific packaging and labels for the waste, and placards on vehicles. The disposal company receiving the waste must also be properly registered with a provincial/state agency to dispose of the specified waste.

Appropriate copies of the hazardous waste shipping manifest must be distributed to the generator, transporter, and receiver of the waste. Documentation must be retained on file for a specified period after disposal. The generator of the waste is responsible for ensuring that:

- disposal is undertaken in a proper manner
- the organizations chosen to transport, dispose of, and/or treat
  the waste are registered with the appropriate provincial/state agency
- the organizations chosen are able to transport or dispose of the waste

Unclassified Wastes

In some jurisdictions, some wastes are not classified as hazardous but may still require special handling in compliance with legislation. Asbestos, for example, must be properly packaged, labeled, and immediately buried after it arrives at an approved landfill site. Salt water from oil well facilities also requires special handling; the salt water must be disposed of by injecting it into a licensed deep well facility.

NOTE

Some government agencies may use the term dangerous waste to classify some wastes. Employees need to know the classification of a waste to determine handling, storage, transportation, and disposal requirements.

Non-hazardous wastes

Non-hazardous wastes are materials which do not meet the classification criteria for hazardous wastes but may still require proper disposal according to company policy or local municipal legislation. Typical non-hazardous wastes include:

- domestic garbage (food wastes, paper, cardboard, wood, etc.)
- non-contaminated industrial wastes (clean concrete, metal, wire, plastic, etc.)
- uncontaminated soils

Non-hazardous materials may be taken to approved landfill sites for disposal or in some jurisdictions they may be recycled.

Hazardous Waste Minimization Practices

Hazardous waste minimization practices—To minimize handling, transporting, and disposal requirements for hazardous wastes, many organizations try to minimize generation of these wastes by applying waste minimization practices, including:

- **reducing** the use of hazardous materials
- **reusing** hazardous materials multiple times before disposal
- **recycling** used hazardous materials through cleaning or re-refining processes. Usually the hazardous materials need to be shipped to recycling facilities for recycle processing.
- **exchanging** wastes with other organizations or sites. A waste material generated from one site may be used for production at another site.

Recycling programs—Recycling programs for hazardous waste materials are regulated. Recycling programs have less onerous transport and documentation requirements than hazardous wastes sent for disposal do. For example, used oils sent for recycling may be transported by company vehicle using standard Transportation of Dangerous Goods (TDG) shipping documents instead of using licensed hazardous waste carriers and hazardous waste manifests. Some jurisdictions do not use TDG manifests; instead, they use manifests specific to their jurisdictions.

LEARNING
ACTIVITY **5**

Safe disposal of wastes

What methods are used to dispose of waste generated by the processes?

How are hazardous and non-hazardous wastes stored and disposed?

5a. Rewrite the question for Issue 5 to suit you, your job, and your workplace. For example, *How can I dispose of the waste properly?* Write your question in the table in the Job Aid at the end of this book.

5b. For your organization, identify a maximum of three wastes that must be transported off-site.

_____

_____

_____

5c. Classify each waste as hazardous, non-hazardous, dangerous, or unclassified.

_____

_____

_____

5d. Select one waste and describe its physical, chemical, and toxicological properties:

physical properties: _____

_____

_____

chemical properties: _____

_____

_____

toxicological properties: _____

_____

_____

_____

5e. Select a waste and identify the location of the MSDS for each hazardous component of the waste.

_____

_____

_____

_____

5f. Select a waste and identify the storage requirements.

_____

_____

5g. For the waste you specified in question 5f, identify the method used to transport the waste off-site.

_____

_____

5h. For the waste you specified in question 5f, identify the disposal method.

_____

_____

5i. Identify the documentation required for transporting and disposal of the waste you identified in question 5f.

_____

_____

5j. Identify applications of waste minimization practices used by your organization.

_____

_____

_____

ISSUE 6	Protecting the environment when there are technical problems

Process Question

Technical	What has to be done to limit the impact that process upsets or equipment failure could have on the environment?
Work	What contingencies can be put in place to deal with unexpected problems or equipment failure that could impact the environment?

Most organizations have contingencies to minimize the impact on the environment should a process upset or equipment failure occur. Some contingencies include:

- reprocessing effluent or emissions
- diverting liquid effluent to storage tanks
- stack flaring to remove pollutants
- installing valves along pipelines to limit the quantity of product released should a leak or rupture occur
- installing double-walled tanks
- building a dike around storage tanks and installing impervious (water resistant) liners
- installing computer-controlled monitoring devices as integral parts of process operation. Computer monitoring and control devices may automatically:
  - adjust equipment operation to control a process upset
  - shut down and isolate equipment should a leak be suspected
  - divert or recycle product
  - activate both audible and visual alarms
- putting in temporary means of containing leaks and spills when working with hazardous products or making repairs to equipment

Quick fix strategies are sometimes used to keep equipment operating or to meet production demands. Some quick fixes can increase risk to the natural environment and personnel. For example:

- adjusting processes to meet production demands could result in an increase in pollution generation

- making temporary maintenance fixes to production or pollution control equipment could increase the potential for the equipment to completely fail

When process upsets occur or equipment fails, the natural environment may be harmed and personnel put at risk. Leaks and spills that occur while performing work or doing maintenance can potentially harm the environment. Therefore, operations and maintenance personnel must be able to efficiently and effectively respond to these types of situations to reduce risk and minimize losses.

Specific policies, practices, and procedures may be established to deal with upsets, abnormal operations, and equipment failure. Employees may receive training to act effectively under normal and abnormal operating and maintenance conditions.

When planning and doing work, consider what can go wrong and the consequences for the environment if an incident occurs. Ask yourself, *What conditions, actions, or events could occur that would have a negative impact on the environment?* If there is a risk of harming the environment, you need to take measures to minimize the potential for an incident to occur and/or minimize the harm that could be done to the environment.

In some cases, an abnormal or upset condition or equipment failure can develop into an emergency condition (Issue 7).

Poor equipment condition can also result in releases to the environment. Note leaks and drips from piping and equipment. Containment systems can be used to contain the product until repairs can be made. Look for indicators of contamination such as:

- sheen on the surface of water
- discolored water
- odors
- stains
- discoloration of equipment, soils, and vegetation
- corrosion
- dying vegetation
- localized weed growth
- erosion

Many organizations store materials that will be consumed in the course of doing business. Materials such as paints, glues, solvents, cleaning solutions, oils, and pesticides must be stored carefully to prevent leaks and, should a leak occur, prevent contamination of the environment. Make sure you know the storage requirements for consumables that can harm the environment.

LEARNING ACTIVITY 6

Protect the environment when there are technical problems

What has to be done to limit the impact that process upsets or equipment could have on the environment?

What contingencies can be put in place to deal with unexpected problems or equipment failure that could impact the environment?

6a. Rewrite the question for Issue 6 to suit you, your job, and your workplace. For example, *How can I minimize the damage if something goes wrong that affects the environment?* Write your question in the table in the Job Aid at the end of this book.

Your organization's activities may or may not involve controlling releases of pollutants into the air, water, or land. If your organization does not release pollutants, work/consult with someone who is involved with technical or work processes that have the potential of harming the environment if something goes wrong.

6b. Within your roles, responsibilities, and job function:

1. Identify the processes where an upset is most likely to occur and that will produce excess pollutants.

_____

_____

_____

2. Identify the equipment that will most likely fail and cause potential harm to the natural environment.

_____

_____

6c. For each identified process upset and equipment failure, identify the contingencies used to minimize damage to the environment.

_____

_____

_____

6d. Identify key personnel that you should communicate with when dealing with process upsets and equipment failures that can have an impact on the natural environment.

_____

_____

_____

6e. Identify the location of the practices and procedures that document the required response to process upsets and equipment failures that could have an impact on the environment.

_____

_____

_____

6f. Identify work processes that have the potential of harming the environment if an incident occurs.

_____

_____

_____

6g. Identify measures that could be taken when doing the work to minimize the potential for an incident to occur and/or minimize the harm that could be done to the environment.

_____

_____

_____

6h. Identify the training required to handle abnormal operations.

_____

_____

_____

6i. Identify three consumable materials that are stored on site that could harm the environment if there was a spill or leak.

_____

_____

_____

6j. Select one material from question 6i and specify how the material is to be stored to prevent contaminating the environment.

_____

_____

_____

ISSUE 7	Minimizing environmental impact when there are emergencies

Process Question

Technical	How does your organization respond to emergencies?
Work	When doing work, what contingencies can be put in place to deal with emergency situations?

An organization must be prepared to respond promptly and effectively to environmental emergencies to ensure environmental damage from a leak or spill is minimized. Government legislation may also require the organization to prepare for other types of emergencies because an emergency situation can have far reaching consequences for the natural environment, human health and safety, facilities, and production. Common types of emergencies which may occur within an organization include:

- accidents which cause severe personal injuries or result in fatalities
- incidents which require rescue operations to be undertaken to protect human life
- releases of chemicals, petroleum products, or other hazardous materials to the environment
- fires or explosions at facilities
- bomb threats or other threats made against personnel or facilities
- natural disasters such as tornadoes, forest fires, floods, earthquakes, tidal waves, or other occurrences which threaten personnel or facilities
- vehicle accidents which cause severe injuries or result in leaks or spills of hazardous materials
- security breaches at facilities
- incidents which require evacuation of personnel from a facility or evacuation of citizens surrounding the facility
- incidents which involve a search for missing or overdue personnel

In any emergency, response actions must be taken to protect:
- the safety of the organization's personnel and the public
- the environment and public and private property

To respond effectively to emergencies, organizations must have an effective emergency response program.

Emergency Response Program

Prompt and effective response to an incident is accomplished through a comprehensive emergency response program which includes:

- assessing, evaluating, and ranking all risks to operations undertaken within the organization
- developing effective spill prevention measures to address risks and to minimize the likelihood of an emergency occurring

- developing written procedures which outline organizational policies and procedures during an emergency
- procuring specialized equipment required to mitigate the effects of an emergency
- training appropriate personnel to ensure they understand their roles and responsibilities and can carry out the required procedures should an emergency occur
- conducting exercises to test equipment and emergency response capabilities
- meeting with outside agencies including the government, other companies, emergency agencies, and the public to share experiences and procedures to improve emergency response capabilities
- incorporating lessons learned during training, exercises, meetings with external stakeholders, and actual incidents to implement safeguards and improved procedures within the organization

Emergency Response Plans

To comply with government legislation and association standards, certain organizations are required to develop emergency response plans. These plans address policies and response actions to be taken in an emergency. Some organizations develop an emergency response manual that addresses all types of emergencies; other organizations develop a separate emergency response manual for specific emergencies.

Some organizations enter into mutual assistance agreements with neighboring organizations. For example, neighboring organizations assist each other in response to fires and spills.

Tests of Emergency Response Plans

At regular intervals, organizations may carry out announced and unannounced simulations of emergencies. Simulations may involve outside agencies such as fire departments, hospitals, and police. The purpose of the simulation is to see how well the organization's emergency response plan works. It takes careful planning to ensure that all employees, on every shift, have an opportunity to participate in simulations.

Incident Investigation and Prevention

When an emergency is over, the incident must be documented. If the environment or personnel safety has been affected, reports must be prepared and forwarded to the proper agencies (Issue 8).

After an incident, the organization often carries out an incident investigation to determine the causes and reasons for the incident. Options to reduce the risk of a similar incident occurring are explored. A cost-benefit assessment may be carried out to select the most appropriate measures to reduce risk. Examples of measures to reduce risk include:

- establishing new policies
- modifying operating and maintenance procedures
- providing training
- upgrading monitoring and control equipment
- redesigning equipment
- changing material specifications

LEARNING ACTIVITY 7

Minimizing environmental impact when there are emergencies

How does the organization respond to emergencies?

When doing work, what contingencies can be put in place to deal with emergency situations?

7a. Rewrite the question for Issue 7 to suit you, your job, and your workplace. For example, *What should I do if there is an emergency?* Write your question in the table in the Job Aid at the end of this book.

Your organization's activities may be of low risk of harming the environment and may not require a comprehensive emergency response plan. If your organization does not have a formal emergency response plan, work/consult with someone whose organization has a formal emergency response plan.

7b. Specify your roles and responsibilities if there is an emergency.

_____

_____

_____

7c. What are the most likely types of emergency that could occur in your organization?

_____

_____

_____

7d. Identify two different types of emergency that could affect your organization and state your first response to each emergency.

_____

_____

_____

7e. What is your preparedness for dealing with emergencies?
Here are some examples:
- you can locate fire and emergency shutdown buttons
- you can locate emergency alarms and interpret audible and visual alarms
- you can locate fire extinguishers, blankets, etc.
- you know the location of the muster areas and the routes to take to get there
- you know the communication requirements during an emergency
- you have first aid training
- you have emergency response training
- you have participated in simulated emergencies

_____

_____

_____

_____

_____

_____

7f. Where are the emergency response manuals located?

_____

_____

_____

7g. Where is the location of specific operating procedures
for performing emergency operational responses such as
shutting down equipment and processes?

_____

_____

_____

| ISSUE 8 | **Keeping informed about organizational activities affecting the environment** |

Process Question

Technical	What environmental reports are required by external agencies?
Work	When doing work, what documentation is required if an incident has a negative impact on the environment?

Government regulations, operating permits, or environmental licenses may require organizations to submit reports on:

- the results from off-site pollution monitoring equipment
- the type and total quantities of air emissions or effluent discharges released to the environment
- quantities of wastes generated at the site
- leaks or spills of hazardous materials
- fires, explosions, and other significant workplace incidents

Results from off-site pollution monitoring equipment must be tabulated and sent to the appropriate government agency on a regular basis. Sometimes, the government may do the monitoring.

Pollutant release reports may require the quantity of products released to be reported in terms of per hour, per day, or per month. All incidents in which the maximum allowable rates were exceeded must normally be identified.

Spills of non-hazardous and hazardous materials (such as oil, refined petroleum products, or regulated chemical compounds) which exceed specific reportable quantities must be reported to appropriate government authorities. Depending on the requirements indicated in the appropriate legislation, reports may be made by telephone or in writing. Follow-up to all actions must also be documented. In many industries, environmental incident reports must be stored for the life of facilities.

If an organization fails to report spills of hazardous materials which exceed reportable quantities, the organization may be fined and their operating licenses and environmental permits may be revoked. Often, operations and maintenance personnel will be the first to notice a spill of hazardous materials. To minimize harm to the natural environment and the public, and the possibility of the organization being fined, all employees must understand their responsibilities to:

• identify spill reporting requirements
• know reportable quantities
• carry out reporting procedures

If the incident has a negative impact on the environment, cleanup and restoration activities may be required (Issue 9).

LEARNING ACTIVITY 8

Keeping informed about organizational activities affecting the environment

What environmental reports are required by external agencies?

When doing work, what documentation is required if an incident has a negative impact on the environment?

8a.   Rewrite the question for Issue 8 to suit you, your job, and your workplace. For example, *Who do I inform and what documentation do I complete if the environment has been affected?* Write your question in the table in the Job Aid at the end of this book.

Your organization may not have activities that can harm the environment should an emergency occur. If that is the case, work/consult with someone whose organization could experience incidents where the environment can be harmed.

For your organization and within your job function:

8b.   Identify the types of environmental monitoring reports that are sent to government agencies.

_____

_____

8c. Identify the job position or person you report to when release rates exceed regulated limits.

_____

_____

_____

8d. Specify your responsibilities for reporting spills of hazardous materials.

_____

_____

_____

8e. State your first response responsibilities when a spill of hazardous materials occurs.

_____

_____

_____

8f. Identify the types of hazardous materials that are most likely to be spilled.

_____

_____

_____

8g. Select two hazardous and/or non-hazardous materials and state the minimum quantity of a spill that must be reported for each material.

_____

_____

_____

8h. Identify the job position or person you must inform when a spill of hazardous materials occurs.

_____

_____

8i.   Identify the location of documents specifying the policies, practices, and procedures for responding to a spill of hazardous materials.

_____

_____

8j.   Identify where to send the spill report documents and who is responsible for sending them.

_____

_____

ISSUE 9	Restoring the environment to its intended use

Process Question

Technical	What environmental clean up or reclamation activities are required?
Work	What can be done to clean up a spill or leak?

Government legislation requires that organizations carry out cleanup, remediation, and reclamation activities as part of doing normal business. Organizations must also clean up in response to uncontrolled incidents that contaminate the environment such as spills of hazardous materials.

Organizations that cease activities involving the extraction of natural resources (e.g., minerals, trees) must carry out restoration activities. When facilities such as gas plants, well sites, pipelines, and roads are permanently decommissioned, the area must be restored to its equivalent capability that existed before being disturbed.

Qualified environmental consultants normally provide assessments and propose remedial measures that are then reviewed and approved by government before being implemented.

Examples of cleanup, remediation, and reclamation activities include:

- cleaning up debris, plowing land, and planting seeds, seedlings, or mature trees after clear cutting of a forested area
- cleaning up site contamination and reclaiming decommissioned mine sites to return the area to a natural state
- reclaiming abandoned oil well sites and industrial manufacturing facilities by removing facilities, remediating contaminated soil and groundwater, and restoring the environment based on the intended land use
- removing tankage at decommissioned service station sites, remediating petroleum contaminated soils and groundwater, and reclaiming the sites for intended use

Spills of hazardous and non-hazardous materials may be cleaned up by contractors or by site personnel. Disposal of the contaminated materials must comply with government regulations.

WARNING

Exposure to hazardous wastes poses health and safety risks. Refer to the Material Safety Data Sheet (MSDS) for a specific substance to get information about hazards and precautions.

Governments may require organizations to make a security deposit for reclamation activities. The purpose of the deposit is to ensure that, if an organization has financial difficulties in the future, funds are available to carry out the reclamation activities.

LEARNING ACTIVITY 9

Restoring the environment to its intended use

What environmental cleanup or reclamation activities are required?

What can be done to clean up a spill or leak?

9a. Rewrite the question for Issue 9 to suit you, your job, and your workplace. For example, *How do I clean up a spill that could affect the environment?* Write your question in the table in the Job Aid at the end of this book.

Because of the nature of your organization's business, there may not be a need for restoration or reclamation. If that is the case, work/consult with someone whose organization could be required to carry out restoration and reclamation activities.

9b.   Identify reclamation activities that your organization has or may have to perform.

_____

_____

_____

9c.   Select one type of spill your organization could experience and describe the methods that would be used to restore the environment to its intended use.

type of spill: _____

_____

_____

_____

9d.   Identify the job position or person in your organization that would be responsible for ensuring spills of hazardous materials are cleaned up satisfactorily.

_____

9e.   Identify the training requirements for spill response.

_____

_____

| ISSUE 10 | **Conserving energy** |

Process Question

Technical	What technical and operational changes can be made to reduce energy use?
Work	What changes can be made to work processes to reduce energy consumption?

Conservation of energy and conservation of materials are closely related—conservation of materials often results in conservation of energy and vice versa. Although conservation methods include waste-minimizing practices (Issue 5), conservation of energy and materials are important enough to be considered as separate environmental issues. When planning and doing work, always consider ways to conserve energy.

Often workers have minimal control over methods to conserve energy because major energy conservation initiatives such as installing additional insulation require large capital investments. However, every person can make small contributions that add up to important gains in conserving energy to reduce the impact on the environment. Two ways to conserve energy are:
- select the source of energy
- reduce the consumption of energy

Selecting the source of energy to reduce the impact on the environment

Energy is harnessed by converting one form of energy into another form. For example:
- coal or natural gas is burned to produce steam which drives turbines to produce rotating mechanical energy. The turbines turn electric generators to produce electricity.
- rivers are dammed to hold back water. The potential energy of the water is converted to kinetic energy that rotates turbines. The turbines drive electrical generators to produce electricity.

- solar panels convert sunlight into electrical energy
- internal combustion engines convert chemical energy into mechanical energy

All methods of harnessing energy impact the environment. Using electric solar panels as an example, each step of their life cycle (cradle to grave) affects the environment:
- mining and transporting raw materials
- refining and transporting refined materials
- producing and transporting semi-finished materials
- producing solar panels and related components
- packaging and transporting solar panels and related components
- handling and storing solar panels and related components
- transporting and installing solar panels and related components
- transporting and disposing of packaging
- maintaining and repairing solar panels and related components
- removing, transporting, and disposing of failed solar panels and related components

Sometimes workers have choices in selecting energy sources to reduce the impact on the environment:
- walking instead of driving
- using a bicycle instead of a vehicle
- driving an electric vehicle instead of one with an internal combustion engine (or a hybrid) provided the electricity has been generated from clean sources such as hydroelectric dams and windmills
- driving a vehicle that runs on natural gas instead of one that runs on gasoline
- car pooling
- plugging into the electric grid instead of using a portable electric generator
- using a portable propane heater versus using a portable electric heater

Consideration must also be given to the efficiency of doing work. For example, many trips with a small electric vehicle may have more of an impact on the environment than making one trip with a gasoline driven vehicle. For portable heaters, converting electricity into heat is less efficient than burning propane. (The electricity may have been produced by burning coal or natural gas in the first place and there is always inefficiency in converting energy from one form to another.)

Reducing energy consumption to minimize the impact on the environment

Technical processes often manipulate variables such as temperature, pressure, flow rate, composition, and reaction time to achieve the desired results. Manufacturing and assembly lines require the coordination of people and equipment to achieve the desired results. Minimizing energy consumption of these types of systems requires careful consideration by specialists such as engineers, health and safety advisors, quality control inspectors, operators, and maintenance personnel. Changes to one part of a system can have adverse affects on other parts of the system. Production, product quality, equipment life, and health and safety of personnel can be affected. Because energy is a cost factor in doing business, an organization may have operating guidelines stating how to operate the systems in ways to minimize energy consumption.

One opportunity to reduce energy consumption and the impact on the environment occurs when equipment needs to be replaced. Equipment may be purchased which is more energy efficient and/or produces less pollution than the equipment in use.

There are often opportunities in work processes to reduce energy consumption. Here are a few examples:
- plan delivery and service routes to minimize the distance traveled
- use the right-sized vehicle to make deliveries. Over-sized vehicles consume more energy.
- plan work activities to minimize travel. For example, several people could car pool to work and to job sites. Materials can be brought to a site and equipment and supplies can be picked up on the return trip.

- use cold or warm water instead of hot water for cleaning
- reduce the room temperature in cold seasons
- reduce the use of air conditioners
- turn off lights and equipment when not in use
- select the right-sized power tools for doing the job
- select methods to do work that require the least amount of energy. For example, instead of cutting plate metal with an acetylene torch, use a shear.
- for equipment that has a specific energy cycle (e.g., autoclave) operate with full loads instead of part loads
- reduce the consumption of materials (Issue 11)

LEARNING ACTIVITY 10

Conserving energy

What technical and operational changes can be made to reduce energy use?

What changes can be made to work processes to reduce energy consumption?

10a. Rewrite the question for Issue 10 to suit you, your job, and your workplace. For example, *How can I conserve energy?* Write your question in the table in the Job Aid at the end of this book.

10b. What could your organization do to reduce energy consumption?

_____

_____

_____

_____

10c. Within your roles, responsibilities, and job function, what can you do to reduce energy consumption?

_____

_____

_____

_____

10d. As an option, identify the impact on the environment of each step in the life cycle of biofuels. Examples of impacts for the first two steps have been provided for you.

Life Cycle of Biofuels	
Action	**Impact**
land use may have been changed from uncultivated land to cultivated land	• changes ecology • could change water drainage patterns
apply fertilizer	• production of fertilizer removes materials from the environment and creates pollution • transportation of fertilizer requires energy and creates pollution • fertilizer application requires energy and creates pollution • fertilizer could drain into water bodies, changing the ecology
sow seed	
produce and transport herbicides and insecticides	
apply herbicides and insecticides	
harvest crop	
store crop	
transport crop to processor	

(continued)

Life Cycle of Biofuels	
Action	Impact
produce biofuel	
transport biofuel to distributor	
travel to distributor to obtain fuel	
consume biofuel	

ISSUE 11	Minimizing material consumption

Process Question

Technical	What technical adjustments can be made to reduce material consumption?
Work	What changes can be made to the work processes to minimize material use?

Reducing material consumption reduces the impact on the environment in several ways:
- reducing the amount of materials removed from the environment
- reducing the amount of waste put back into the environment
- reducing the amount of energy required to produce and transport the material thereby reducing pollution

Minimizing practices are often applied:
- **reduce** the use of materials (or maximize the use of materials to minimize waste)
- **reuse** materials multiple times before disposal
- **recycle** used materials through cleaning or re-refining processes
- **exchange** wastes with other organizations or sites

Some suggestions of ways to reduce consumption are listed below.

Minimize waste (maximize use) of materials

- order materials (e.g., lumber, drywall) of the right size
- when using sheet materials (e.g., plywood) do pattern layouts to maximize the use of materials
- control the amount of material used to maintain the minimum required amount. For example:
  - apply paints, sealers, and floor surfacing materials to the recommended amount and no more
  - carefully prepare the grade of driveways and parking lots to minimize the use of asphalts and concrete
  - rotate products that have a shelf life so that the oldest products get used first
  - organize the application of coatings in a way that minimizes the amount of equipment cleaning required (i.e., apply a color or type of coating to as many surfaces as possible before changing to a different color or product)
  - repair leaks

Extend the use of materials

- solvents used for cleaning parts and tools can be divided into two batches—a dirty batch and a clean batch. Use the dirty solvent for the first cleaning step and the clean solvent for the final cleaning. Continue using the dirty solvent until it is no longer effective. When the clean solvent becomes dirty, use it for the first cleaning step.
- use rags and scrapers to physically remove large amounts of dirt, paints, and other coating materials from parts and tools before using solvents
- use settling tanks to clean solvents and machinery coolants. Periodically clean out the sludge to extend product life.
- use recycled materials (e.g., brick, lumber) instead of new materials
- replace throw-away consumables with products that can be cleaned and reused (e.g., replace disposable plastic drapes with cloth drapes)
- extend the life of consumables by cleaning (e.g., wash gloves, sponges, hoses)
  - use consumables to their maximum use (e.g., continue to

use rags, toweling, and sponges for cleaning until they
are saturated)

– maximize the functional life of consumables. For
example, often maintenance will change oil and filters
according to equipment use or schedule. An oil analysis
may prove that the oil change schedule can be extended.

– substitute a product with a short life span with a product
that has a longer life span. For example, one oil may be
replaced by another oil that lasts longer. The upgrade
may be more cost-effective.

– put a spent product to a different use (e.g., water used to
rinse off equipment could be captured and used to water
the lawn)

Exchange wastes

- seek out organizations that produce a consistent type of
waste that your organization can use (e.g., ends of lumber
cut off at a consistent length by one organization could be
used by another organization to make planters)
- seek out organizations that can use a consistent type of
waste that your organization produces
- sell used materials (e.g., doors from renovations)

LEARNING ACTIVITY 11

Minimizing material consumption

*What technical adjustments can be made to reduce
material consumption?*

*What changes can be made to the work processes to
minimize material use?*

11a. Rewrite the question for Issue 11 to suit you, your job,
and your workplace. For example, *How can I maximize
the use of materials?* Write your question in the table in
the Job Aid at the end of this book.

11b. What could your organization do to reduce material
consumption?

_____

_____

_____

11c. Within your roles, responsibilities, and job function, what can you do to reduce the use of materials and minimize consumption?

_____

_____

_____

_____

Summary of the Critical Thinking Strategy to Protect the Environment

Organizations use various environmental management strategies to ensure that their activities do not harm the environment. As part of an environmental protection strategy, every person in the organization has a responsibility to protect the natural environment.

Documented policies, practices, and procedures are useful in providing you with directions that minimize harm to the environment. Using the critical thinking strategy to identify and respond to environmental issues relating to your job can also help you meet your responsibilities. The strategy described in this book involves asking eleven questions relating to environmental issues. The following table lists the environmental issues and related questions.

The first question is the most important one to ask to determine if there is an impact on the natural environment. You want to determine if there are any activities that remove, modify, or add to air, water, or land.

If the answer is yes to the first question, then the other questions logically follow. Not all of the questions may apply to a given job. For example, if the answer is no to the first question, several other questions are not relevant.

For work processes, the questions can be used before, during, and after completing the work. The first question is an important one to ask before starting work. While doing the work, consider the consequences for the natural environment of a condition, action, or event. Also, determine the environmental reasons for particular steps of a procedure. After the work has been completed, consider how the conditions or possible events could affect the environment.

To help you remember the questions, you reworked each one (in the table in the Job Aid at the end of this book) to suit you, your particular type of work, and job applications. Memorize these questions so that you work effectively in ways that protect the environment and are prepared to respond effectively to environmental incidents.

Critical Thinking Strategy to Protect the Environment		
Environmental Issue	Technical Process Question	Work Process Question
1. Impact on the natural environment	Does the process have the potential to affect the environment?	Is there anything that can cause harm to the environment?
2. Pollutant release rates	What are the allowable pollutant release rates and quantities?	How much material can be released, disposed, or harvested without harming the environment?
3. Measuring and monitoring pollutant releases	How are pollutant releases measured or monitored?	What are the types and specifications of the equipment used to measure and monitor pollutant releases?
4. Controlling the impact on the environment	What technical controls are being used to limit environmental impact?	What are the types and specifications of the equipment used to limit the impact on the environment?
5. Safe disposal of wastes	What methods are used to dispose of wastes generated by the processes?	How are hazardous and non-hazardous wastes stored and disposed?
6. Protecting the environment when there are technical problems	What has to be done to limit the impact that process upsets or equipment failure could have on the environment?	What contingencies can be put in place to deal with unexpected problems or equipment failure that could impact the environment?
7. Minimizing environmental impact when there are emergencies	How does your organization respond to emergencies?	When doing work, what contingencies can be put in place to deal with emergency situations?
8. Keeping informed about organizational activities affecting the environment	What environmental reports are required by external agencies?	When doing work, what documentation is required if an incident has a negative impact on the environment?
9. Restoring the environment to its intended use	What environmental cleanup or reclamation activities are required?	What can be done to clean up a spill or leak?

(continued)

EnviroThink™

Critical Thinking Strategy to Protect the Environment		
Environmental Issue	**Technical Process Question**	**Work Process Question**
10. Conserving energy	What technical and operational changes can be made to reduce energy use?	What changes can be made to work processes to reduce energy consumption?
11. Minimizing material consumption	What technical adjustments can be made to reduce material consumption?	What changes can be made to the work processes to minimize material use?

Environmental Standards

Many different organizations and agencies have taken initiatives to protect the environment.

Legislation

Governments establish environmental standards and guidelines to protect and manage the environment in the jurisdictions they govern. Environmental legislation may be enacted at the federal, provincial/state, and municipal government levels and can cover a broad range of issues including:

- approval processes for industry to construct and operate new facilities
- environmental impact assessment procedures for new facilities
- environmental auditing practices and procedures
- monitoring processes and release limits for potential pollutants
- methods and controls for storing, transporting, and disposing of waste
- storage and transportation of hazardous products (land, rail, air, and water)

- environmental impact assessment procedures for contaminated sites
- reporting requirements for environmental accidents and spills
- emergency response requirements and procedures for accidents and spills
- contaminated site reclamation and restoration procedures
- compliance requirements and enforcement procedures

Legislative requirements for each facility will differ according to the types of operation undertaken and the extent of the environmental impact. Regulatory requirements for a facility may include environmental operating permits, licenses, or regulatory requirements identified in legislation. Specific information required may include limits for discharge of pollutants, required monitoring to be undertaken, and deadlines or time limits for reporting.

Agencies and Associations

Government agencies, professional associations, and organizations whose guidelines are recognized worldwide have established standards for environmental protection.

World Health Organization (WHO), an arm of the United Nations, provides practical standards for human health such as acceptable standards for drinking water.

Most countries have federal environmental agencies such as Environment Canada. The United States Environmental Protection Agency (USEPA) has member associations throughout the world. This association provides guidelines for concentrations of contaminants in air, water, and land.

In Canada, the Canadian Council of Ministers of the Environment (CCME) has developed and published environmental guidelines for assessing environmental risk, environmental management, and environmental auditing.

In Europe, the European Environment Agency (EEA) provides a wide range of services such as studies and information to its members. The agency focuses on four general areas:

- climate change
- biodiversity loss and understanding spatial change
- human health and quality of life
- use and management of natural resources and waste

International trade organizations and agreements such as the World Trade Organization (WTO) and the North America Free Trade Agreement (NAFTA) also have an influence on environmental policies.

Local industrial associations such as oil and gas and pulp and paper associations have also developed environmental standards, policies, and practices. Association members can adopt these standards as part of their internal environmental management programs.

ISO 14000

The International Organization for Standardization (ISO) has developed the ISO 14000 series of standards to guide large and small organizations on how to manage their business activities, processes, products, and services more effectively to achieve environmental objectives. ISO 14001 maps out the policy, planning, implementation, checking, and review mechanisms required in an environmental management system. Though ISO guidelines are voluntary, ISO certification is increasingly becoming a requirement of organizations to do business with other organizations. In some cases, a company may become certified because it believes that its certified competitors have an advantage.

Responsible Care

The International Council of Chemical Associations (ICCA) oversees Responsible Care®.

Responsible Care is a program conceived by the Canadian Chemical Producers' Association (CCPA) in 1984. Responsible Care's main objectives are to improve the chemical industry's environmental, health, and safety performance; improve the industry's relationship with communities and government; and encourage the development of public trust. Responsible Care is broader and more comprehensive than ISO 14000.

Whereas ISO 14000 focuses on management systems to achieve environmental goals, Responsible Care focuses on management practices that address health, safety, and environmental issues.

Responsible Care®

The American Chemistry Council (ACC) has registered the name Responsible Care®.

Responsible Care programs have been adapted by industry associations in over 40 countries. The guiding principles of Responsible Care apply to all programs; the programs of individual countries, however, may have different emphases. Responsible Care programs have six to eight management codes of practice, depending on the emphasis and on how the chemical association of a country chooses to define a code of practice. The codes of practice cover:

- community right to know
- community awareness and emergency response
- research and development
- process safety
- employee health and safety
- pollution prevention
- hazardous waste management
- warehousing and storage
- transportation
- distribution
- product stewardship

Although Responsible Care programs are voluntary, association members are required to set stringent standards and provide proof (verification) of compliance with the codes of practice and implementation activities.

Organizations who implement a Responsible Care program can realize both financial and operational benefits. Benefits include:

- reduced employee incidents and accidental releases of pollutants
- improved customer satisfaction
- development of positive relationships with communities, government agencies, and manufacturers

One of the guiding principles of Responsible Care is the commitment to continuous performance improvement in all aspects of health, safety, and environment. In keeping with the spirit of continuous improvement, the Responsible Care program itself is also continually evolving.

In some government jurisdictions, when organizations are planning to expand or build new facilities, organizations submit their standards to different levels of government for approval rather than have the government impose standards. Organizations that have comprehensive health, safety, and environmental programs, such as Responsible Care, are in a better position to have their proposals approved because these organizations have stringent standards.

In addition to complying with various environmental regulations and standards established by governments, agencies, and associations, organizations may develop specific internal policies and procedures to achieve their environmental objectives.

Job Aid

Environmental Issue	Question
1. Impact on the natural environment	
2. Pollutant release rates	
3. Measuring and monitoring pollutant releases	
4. Controlling the impact on the environment	
5. Safe disposal of wastes	
6. Protecting the environment when there are technical problems	

(continued)

EnviroThink™

Environmental Issue	Question
7. Minimizing environmental impact when there are emergencies	
8. Keeping informed about organizational activities affecting the environment	
9. Restoring the environment to its intended use	
10. Conserving energy	
11. Minimizing material consumption	

Another book by Gordon D. Shand

Interviewing to Gather Relevant Content for Training

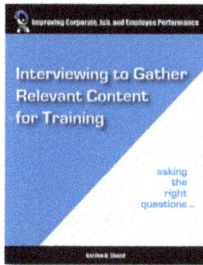

Effective training contributes to business success— **improved corporate, job, and employee performance**. But how do you figure out what training is effective? This book provides the strategies you need to identify training that will give you the best return on your investment in training.

Part A:
- provides criteria and strategies you can use to identify:
  - training content that is relevant
  - what content you should address and not address
- describes pitfalls that you can encounter and ways to resolve these pitfalls

Part B describes an interviewing process where you provide leadership to identify and gather content that is relevant, useful, and practical. You will learn how to:
- help the subject matter expert provide quality content
- select content that is relevant and eliminate content that will not improve performance
- keep the subject matter expert engaged
- structure the content to effectively and efficiently develop training and assessment resources

The suggestions in this book are the accumulated experiences of many training and performance consultants who have encountered the challenges of gathering relevant content and developing effective training.

Who can benefit?

- educational, training, and performance consultants
- training program designers
- instructional designers
- technical writers
- trainers and coaches
- internal staff who develop training

www.ingramcontent.com/pod-product-compliance
Lightning Source LLC
Chambersburg PA
CBHW051556030426

42334CB00034B/3453